Praise for *The Planet You Inherit:*
Letters to My Grandchildren When Uncertainty's a Sure Thing

"There's real wisdom in this book, not just for the next generation but for those of us making the decisions right now. Those of us of a certain age have a very real responsibility to do *everything* we can to pass on a working planet to those who come after!"

—Bill McKibben, Schumann Distinguished Scholar, Middlebury College, and author of *The Flag, the Cross, and the Station Wagon: A Graying American Looks Back at His Suburban Boyhood and Wonders What the Hell Happened*

"*The Planet You Inherit* is a profound offering of wisdom and love, imparted by one of the preeminent ethicists of our time to his own grandchildren. What a blessing that we are invited to listen in, absorbing colorful pieces of history, mind-expanding glimpses of metaphysics, and a bedrock case for cultivating those 'bonds of love and belonging' that are essential to life. Beautifully written, unflinchingly honest, and deeply personal, this book is a guide for all who seek to live a full and moral life in this unprecedented time in which 'we are not only the ark but the flood.'"

—Karenna Gore, author, activist, and executive director of the Center for Earth Ethics at Union Theological Seminary

"Larry Rasmussen has written a wise and compassionate book, precisely the sort of book our Anthropocene world needs. Don't let the title fool you. This is a book for young people, but it is also for all adults who now (and quickly) need to learn the art of becoming good ancestors."

—Norman Wirzba, Gilbert T. Rowe Distinguished Professor of Theology, Duke University, and author of *This Sacred Life: Humanity's Place in a Wounded World*

"Larry Rasmussen is one of the few great Christian ethicists of the last half-century. This profound and powerful text to the younger generation is a gem!"

—Cornel West, Dietrich Bonhoeffer Professor of Philosophy and Christian Practice, Union Theological Seminary

"Larry Rasmussen has created a unique collection of letters that will resonate not only with his grandchildren but with all those seeking a way forward through the climate emergency. To have anxiety about the future of the Earth community is to be awake in a broken world. Larry shows us how we might navigate this with empathy, compassion, and courage."

—Mary Evelyn Tucker and John Allen Grim, Yale Forum on Religion and Ecology

"Writing to his own with unabashed affection and sober realism, Earth-honoring ethicist Larry Rasmussen pours out a lifetime of environmental knowledge, prophetic witness, and personal experience. His letters will inspire the rising generation—and the older folks reading over their shoulders—to ever-bolder love for this precious biosphere, its unjustly divided inhabitants, and the Living Presence that sustains all things and summons us to responsibility. As human generations and geological ages turn, this book is a gift to all Earth's grandchildren, and to the adults who love them."

—Mark R. Schwehn and Dorothy C. Bass, grandparents of six and coeditors of *Leading Lives That Matter: What We Should Do and Who We Should Be*

"The relationship between generations, especially between grandparent and grandchild, is essential to the path ahead. The open-eyed wonder of childhood, in tandem with age's studied wisdom, is exactly what we need. *The Planet You Inherit* models the way forward for us all. It is a book of extraordinary hope in a time of urgent need."

—John Philip Newell, author of *Sacred Earth, Sacred Soul*

"Many of us thirst to hear about the climate emergency in a manner that sparks imagination; places us wide-awake in a future defined by displacement and vulnerability; breaks, opens, and activates our hearts to care and do more. These letters from Grandpa, whom many of us cherish as Prof. Larry Rasmussen, do this humanizing work justly and with fearful grace."

—Rev. Fletcher Harper, executive director of GreenFaith

"With the patient 'speed of love,' Dr. Rasmussen recounts the hope, humility, and inspiration that can be found in evolutionary history, philosophy, theology, politics, and ethics, all conveyed with tender compassion and inspired conviction. In a world fraught with violence, fear, and despair, Larry's love letter is a manifesto for a moral revolution."

—William P. Brown, William Marcellus McPheeters Professor of Old Testament, Columbia Theological

Seminary, and author of *The Seven Pillars of Creation: The Bible, Science, and the Ecology of Wonder* and *Deep Calls to Deep: The Psalms in Dialogue amid Disruption*

"This is a must-read for grandparents and grandchildren and those who are still to be. It is beautifully written and sent with love, but its message is urgent and compelling. Our planet is in deep trouble. There is still much we can do to turn things around if we wake up and do not lose hope."

—Isobel and John de Gruchy, grandparents, artists, and authors of books on Julian of Norwich and Dietrich Bonhoeffer

"These are love letters in the truest sense—full of wisdom, wonder, radical honesty, and lament, written to Rasmussen's grandsons with poignant tenderness. These letters are also an opportunity to sit at the knee of some of the wisest and most influential people of our time—James Baldwin and Maya Angelou, Dietrich Bonhoeffer and Reinhold Niebuhr, Albert Einstein and Robin Wall Kimmerer. Perhaps most importantly, these letters are about cultivating and living out faith, hope, and love in our beautiful yet imperiled world."

—Jim Martin-Schramm, professor emeritus of religion, Luther College, and Karen Martin-Schramm, retired executive assistant to the president, Luther College

"These letters are for all of us, so sit down and let the stories unfold. Many times the stories are not easy and carry the anxiety of our time. But they also prepare us to face our fears, offering ways through our climate disasters with hope and imagination. Thank you, Larry, for these stories."

—Cláudio Carvalhaes, associate professor of worship, Union Theological Seminary, and author of *Ritual at World's End*

"These letters speak beauty—the beauty of searing truth spoken, the beauty of a heart burst open in delight and lament, the beauty of words crafted with exquisite grace. Here we breathe wonder, piercing honesty, and profound hope. This is poetry in prose form, science in the garb of wonder, and prayer as life's gratitude. *The Planet You Inherit* is culminating testimony of a profoundly wise theologian, mystic, artist, and lover of life."

—Cynthia Moe-Lobeda, professor of theological and social ethics, and director of the Center for Climate Justice and Faith, Pacific Lutheran Theological Seminary, and author of *Resisting Structural Evil: Love as Ecological-Economic Vocation*

"*The Planet You Inherit* is a profound work of love, courage, and wisdom. Courage to speak a hard truth with full honesty and to grieve momentous responsibility and loss. A grandfather's love that cares beyond measure for this living planet as he cares for his own grandchildren."

—Rabbi Nahum Ward-Lev, author of *The Liberating Path of the Hebrew Prophets: Then and Now*

"All books by Larry Rasmussen feature his wonderful blend of encyclopedic knowledge, judicious analysis, and poetic beauty, but this one is a distinct gift: an updated *Earth-Honoring Faith* in the form of love letters to Larry's grandchildren. This luminous gift will be gratefully received for many years to come, if there are many years to come."

—Gary Dorrien, Reinhold Niebuhr Professor of Social Ethics, Union Theological Seminary, New York City, and author of *In a Post-Hegelian Spirit: Philosophical Theology as Idealistic Discontent*

"Writing to his grandchildren, Rasmussen represents all of us grappling with the regret and trauma of our times. In the new age of instability, Rasmussen, like Bonhoeffer, finds sure hope (rather than glib optimism) in community, honesty, and love for others. It is a profound and beautiful companion as we learn to live in the Anthropocene."

—Dr. Dianne Rayson, University of Newcastle, School of Humanities, Creative Industries and Social Sciences, and author of *Bonhoeffer and Climate Change: Theology and Ethics for the Anthropocene*

"In *The Planet You Inherit* Larry Rasmussen offers wise counsel for living in perilous times, distilled from a lifetime of teaching ethics. These love letters from Holocene grandparents to their Anthropocene grandchildren are vintage Rasmussen, deeply insightful and graced with gentle humor—a compass for living into the future with faith and hope. In years to come we will bequeath this road map for living well in uncertain times to our grandchildren, while heeding its message today."

—Dan Spencer and Pat Burke, University of Montana, and grandparents to Colin, Meghan, and Maverick

"For decades Larry Rasmussen has been warning tens of thousands through his insightful lectures and gifted writing about the epoch-changing perils posed by climate change. But his most persuasive and poignant message of all is delivered to two people—his grandchildren—through this book."

—Wesley Granberg-Michaelson, author of *Without Oars: Casting Off into a Life of Pilgrimage*, and general secretary emeritus of the Reformed Church in America

"Our kids and his grandkids will inherit a drastically changed Earth, but we hope they also inherit Rasmussen's resilient faith in the creative restlessness of the human spirit, his passion for justice for the poor and the Earth, and his 'giddy love of unexpected life' that exudes sheer gratitude for the beauty and joy of this astounding cosmos."

—Dan and Anna Scheid, theological ethicists, authors, associate professors at Duquesne University, and parents of three children

"What a gift to sit with love letters informed by science, life stories, and spiritual grounding in wonder, mystery, and hope. We need this spiritually informed foundation to live into the future. I believe Larry Rasmussen has just adopted thousands more grandchildren through this book of reality, hope, and love."

—Joan Brown, Catholic Franciscan sister and executive director, New Mexico & El Paso Region Interfaith Power and Light; honored in 2015 as a White House Champion of Change for climate justice work

"How fortunate we are to be invited into this intimate conversation between a wise elder and his young grandchildren, sharing with radical honesty the tragic dimension of life while teaching us all how to say 'yes to life in spite of everything.' Larry Rasmussen issues a clarion call to courageous, responsible action on behalf of a suffering, sacred world. Written for those who will inherit an altered Earth and uncharted human future, these are 'love letters from first to last,' where wonder has the final word."

—Rev. Robyn Hartwig, pastor and organizer of EcoFaith Recovery, and Rev. Dr. Janet Parker, engagement coordinator with EcoFaith Recovery

"This collection of letters is at once a summation of the major themes of Larry's work, an accessible body of moral teaching to offer all who are willing to learn, and a beautiful offering of love to his beloved grandchildren. And his beloved country. And his beloved cosmos. This book is a benediction. I respond by saying: Amen."

—David Gushee, professor of Christian ethics, Mercer University and Free University Amsterdam, and grateful grandfather of Jonah and Melody

"These moving and loving letters to his grandchildren speak to them and to us with powerful images of the destruction of the earth that we are sowing and an unyielding hope that we can live into justice-making and earth-keeping to stop this curse. Read with care."

—Emilie M. Townes, distinguished professor of womanist ethics and society, Vanderbilt University Divinity School

THE PLANET YOU INHERIT

THE PLANET YOU INHERIT

Letters to My Grandchildren When Uncertainty's a Sure Thing

LARRY L. RASMUSSEN

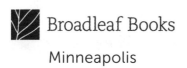

Broadleaf Books

Minneapolis

THE PLANET YOU INHERIT
Letters to My Grandchildren When Uncertainty's a Sure Thing

Graph used with permission from Science, Vol. 339, p. 1198: A reconstruction of regional and global temperature for the last 11,300 years.

Levertov Poem. *Denise Levertov New Selected Poems* (Bloodaxe Books, 2003). Reproduced with permission of Bloodaxe Books. www.bloodaxebooks.com

Text for *In All Our Living/Pues si vivimos* reproduced with permission of the United Methodist Publishing House.

Cover image: Pexel.com
Cover design: Katie Lukes

Print ISBN: 978-1-5064-7353-6
eBook ISBN: 978-1-5064-7354-3

THESE LETTERS ARE DEDICATED TO

Eduardo Rasmussen Villegas;
Martín Rasmussen Villegas;
Liv Noelle Diers Parsons;
John Asante Harris;
Madison, Camille, and Asher Merryman;
and their loving parents.

Eduardo Rasmussen Villegas and Martín
Rasmussen Villegas, 2020

CONTENTS

FOREWORD

Terry Tempest Williams

Letters of Consequence

When Nelson Mandela first came to the United States in the summer of 1990, after being released from serving twenty-seven years in prison, his number one priority was to visit New York City. He wanted to thank the churches for the divestment campaign from South Africa in America. That campaign's beginning lay with graduate students at Union Theological Seminary. Larry Rasmussen was one of those students.

During his time as a PhD student at Union (from 1965 to 1968), Larry was part of a group that decided to transfer their personal bank account funds from Chemical Bank, a large New York bank that was making loans to the apartheid government of South Africa, to the new Freedom National Bank on 125th Street in Harlem, an institution that came out of the civil rights movement. The president of the bank was Jackie Robinson. Larry would tell you his transfer, along with the dozen or so students, included a balance of "two digits left of the period." That wasn't what mattered. What mattered is that they took a stand and that stand grew as they talked to other church organizations to follow suit and boycott US banks loaning money to South Africa. Soon other organizations were joining the anti-apartheid divestment movement with true momentum arriving when the California teacher's pension fund joined the movement.

In Larry Rasmussen's words, "In a victory for us, Union Seminary also withdrew its accounts from Chemical Bank and put their money in Freedom National. And I remember the packed sanctuary at the Riverside Church when Nelson Mandela, released from prison but not yet elected president of a non-apartheid South Africa, mounted the pulpit to thank the churches across the country for the Divestment Campaign."

Rasmussen had been at the Riverside Church before on April 4, 1967, when Martin Luther King Jr. delivered his landmark speech, "A Time to Break Silence." One can imagine Larry seated in that house of worship with his peers from Union listening to these words spoken by Reverend King:

> I'm in deepest agreement with the aims and work of the organization which has brought us together: Clergy and Laymen Concerned About Vietnam. . . . I found myself in full accord when I read [the statement's] opening lines: "A time comes when silence is betrayal." And some of us who have already begun to break the silence of the night have found that the calling to speak is often a vocation of agony, but we must speak. . . . [We] religious leaders have chosen to move . . . to the high grounds of a firm dissent based on the mandates of conscience and the reading of history.

Larry Rasmussen took those words and placed them inside his soul and acted on them. "Ten days after the Riverside address," he writes, "we all marched with King from Central Park to the United Nations." History reports Dr. King spoke before a crowd of 125 thousand people, urging the United Nations to pressure the United States to stop bombing Vietnam.

From protesting the Vietnam War to supporting the civil rights movement that led to his own actions of helping to organize the Anti-Apartheid Movement in America as a student at Union; to his own moral merging of social justice with environmental justice; to the intersectionality of human and ecological survival inherent within the climate crisis before us that he so powerfully speaks to now—the moral trajectory of Larry Rasmussen can be traced through these loving letters found in *The Planet You Inherit* written to his grandsons, Eduardo and Martin. It is here in these insightful pages that Larry Rasmussen says to his grandsons, citing Viktor Frankel, "Being conscious is simply being alive. And being both alive and responsible is the truth of being human."

Amen.

There are few people in the world I admire more than Larry Rasmussen. He is a peacemaker, a spiritual leader who walks the path led by Dr. Martin Luther King Jr. and Nelson Mandela, men he admired, whom he followed, walked with, and worked for their principles of freedom and justice for all. He speaks the truth from the vantage point of a long, full life committed to social and ecological justice. Larry has devoted his whole being to an ethical stance toward life. He is a pioneering force in the now burgeoning realm of eco-theology that includes justice for *all species* and their right to live and flourish on earth. Whereas, environmentalists tended to ignore human injustices in relationship to the injustices to the land; and the social justice movement primarily focused on human needs outside of their interconnectedness with the environment, Larry Rasmussen, as the Reinhold Niebuhr Professor Emeritus of Social Ethics at Union Theological Seminary, brings these two hands of concern together in prayer.

This same prayer for a just world can be heard and, most importantly, felt in this deeply moving book *The Planet You Inherit: Letters to My Grandchildren When Uncertainty's a Sure Thing*. The letters are penned to his grandsons, Eduardo and Martin, now children, to be read throughout their lives. Larry and his beloved companion, Nyla, have embraced not only their own children and grandchildren but all of us for whom they have so generously brought into their loving circle of community, a community of care and joy.

Larry Rasmussen, as grandfather to Eduardo and Martin, writes in his letter on October 18, 2020, "What's patently unfair is that you, as Anthropocene kids, did not create the problems you're inheriting, yet you're forced to be responsible for them throughout your lives. The question is not whether you will have to confront climate catastrophe but how you will respond, individually and collectively." He encourages them to find "your vocation, your calling, your Great Work" that "will be to remap the world on an altered Earth for a different way of life in an uncharted future." He then says, "I suspect you will find yourself 'saying yes to life in spite of everything.'"

The Planet You Inherit is a rich compendium of information, history, and wisdom. It is not without its tools for retrieving what we may have lost: hope. These letters are for anyone in search of a map that might better illuminate where we are and how we got here. I keep returning to the letter written on

February 26, 2021. Rasmussen speaks of "essential elements needed to thrive in the Anthropocene." "We'll build cairns," he tells Eduardo and Martin. "Cairns are small stone towers that serve as points of reference where the trail doesn't yet exist or is easily lost." I now look for the cairns that Larry has set forth on this uncertain path we now all share as human beings: cosmology, community, ethics, and ritual. He defines the last cairn as the inner journey, "the vital role of cultivating spirituality for life in a new epoch." What we see through these letters written by one of our elders at this moment in time, is that the challenges we face are not just political issues or social issues or even environmental issues, but spiritual ones. Larry Rasmussen embodies what a spiritual life in the name of love, family, and community can yield when we choose to be in the service of something larger than ourselves.

Ralph Waldo Emerson's saying comes to mind: "The purpose of life is not to be happy. It is to be useful, to be honorable, to be compassionate, to have it make some difference that you have lived and lived well."

The Planet You Inherit is more than an epistolary; it is a call to loving action, arm in arm with others, on this beautiful, broken planet we call home.

Terry Tempest Williams
Harvard Divinity School
February 28, 2022

AUTHOR'S NOTE

I knew my grandchildren confronted the harrowing challenge of moving from industrial to ecological civilization. *The Great Transition*, it's called. Epic times.

I was ready for that. But my pen was startled to discover a truth that's taken us by stealth: That for the first time ever, humanity's become a geological force. We've slid off the back end of one geological epoch, the Holocene, onto the front end of another, the Anthropocene. The Age of the Human. Thus, we face epoch times as well as epic times and a further daunting transition.

These transitions are the Great Work (Thomas Berry) that awaits my grandchildren. Though they were never asked and didn't get a vote, remapping and remaking the world amid uncertainty is their calling, as it is ours. Although their world cannot be ours, and shouldn't be, I wanted to step away from an academic career teaching social ethics and just write love letters—love letters that face what they face on a changed and changing planet. I'm certain the letters are urgent. Not because the kids' grandparents are frail but because their world is.

EPOCH TIMES

Dear Eduardo,

This is a love letter. But not the usual kind. Of course, your Grandma Nyla and I, along with your *abuelos* in Colombia, match doting grandparents anywhere. Our affection lacks nothing.

Yet this is the very first letter in the whole history of love that consciously sends love from grandparents in one geological epoch to a grandchild in another—from the late Holocene to the early Anthropocene.

That's weird. It's also important because the Anthropocene is the time of your life, while the Holocene is the time of ours.

To us, this language is strange. Yet probably not to you if you are reading this as a young adult. (Now you're still a preschooler, so I expect you won't read this for many years.) Unlike us, you will experience the tumultuous changes that straddle a new geological epoch. Although human history and human experience were our main subjects, earth science and planetary experience will likely be yours. Our human drama is a chapter in Earth's drama, and Earth's drama is a chapter in the galaxy's. We belong to the journey of the universe.

I awoke this morning to write of your geological epoch and mine. I suspect you already know from school and your smartwatch that *Holocene* means "the wholly recent" epoch (ours), while *Anthropocene* (yours) means "the age of the human"—from *anthropos,* Greek for "human." (God only knows why all geologists speak Greek.)

It's hopelessly nerdy to include a graph. What love letter features a science graph?

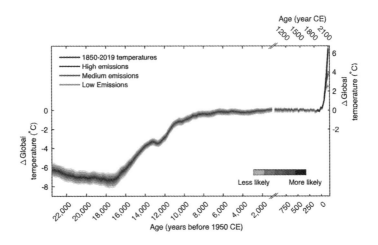

Follow the line. From the last eleven thousand years to zero—the late Holocene. The variation is less than 1°C (1.7°F) above the baseline to less than one degree below it. This small two-degree Celsius difference is rare in Earth's history. Look how erratic the line is before it flattens. Earth is normally fickle.

Here's the kicker. The grammar of the epoch that has hosted every single human civilization to date, bar none, comes down to climate stability—uncommon stability generating a riot of life. And it's coming to an end.

It's more than climate, though. The whole natural world is uncommonly reliable in the late Holocene. Friendly, too, by comparison. That tranquility—predictable seasons—made agriculture possible, as well as settled societies and cities. There could be divisions of labor and social stratification, along with domesticated plants and animals, all because people lived in places with dependable habitats. It's not a coincidence that the earliest civilizations all arose at the same time, whether in China, India, Egypt, Persia, or Mexico, courtesy of a friendly Holocene.

How important is that to who you are? Our brand of humans—*Homo sapiens*—has been marching around and making love for two hundred thousand to three hundred thousand years. But *sapien* civilizations have only existed for the past ten thousand to twelve thousand years. Since we had big brains, native intelligence, and lots of life experience long before any civilizations arose, why the delay of a couple hundred thousand years? Why is civilization an exception, even for us? Because settled societies had to wait until the big ice sheets receded to the poles and a long stretch of climate moderation settled in. All settled societies developed within a narrow temperature band.

So if "the only period as stable *as* our own *is* our own," as one climate journalist put it, and climate stability is a prerequisite for organized society, what do we do now when planetary uncertainty's the only sure thing?

Grandma Nyla's and my lifetime fall to the far right of this line, where the line heads straight up. That spike is the early Anthropocene epoch. It's where we leave our lives behind and you begin yours. Did you know that before your generation, no humans of any stripe ever lived on a planet as hot as this one?

I cannot tell you what we would give so that you did not live your days on that trajectory. That line—your life—is climate *in*stability, mass uncertainty, and breathtaking extinction. Tragedy crouches there, and I pray that somehow you wring adaptation from distress. A stone sits in my stomach because I know that Anthropocene citizens who continue Holocene habits doom their children.

Still, the world has not stopped being beautiful. You will remember our days on the red rock mesas of New Mexico, "this beautiful broken country of erosional beauty where rocks tell time differently and the wing beats of ravens come to us as prayers." You'll remember our adobe-style house, too, and many patio hours sketching with colored chalk or doing a puzzle together. You may also remember dark skies of bright stars, even here in town, and the blue and pink stripes on the horizon at dawn.

I guess the Greeks had it right. Their word *cosmos* means "order"—those stars in their courses—and it also means "beauty," as in *cosmetics*, though *cosmetics* is a bit trivial for the life and death of a hundred billion galaxies! Or for a striped dawn.

Cosmos as beauty and order belongs to life, Eduardo, so go Greek and claim the beauty that exists. Let it guide you. Beauty is its own resistance, contending with all that is ugly and chaotic.

Alice Walker is my favorite on this. The sentence that gave her most famous novel its title finds Shug saying, "I think it pisses God off if you walk by the color purple in a field somewhere and don't notice it." That's how we should walk, with our step affected by beautiful things like the color purple. Pissing God off isn't a good idea, either.

If the tumultuous world has not stopped being beautiful, neither has love stopped being love: "Even a wounded world is feeding us. Even a wounded world holds us, giving us moments of wonder and joy." That's my latest most favorite author, Robin Wall Kimmerer, and she's right: if we choose joy over despair and love over hate, it's because Earth offers love and joy daily.

In any event, you, Grandma Nyla, and I have precious days together in the great transition that will define every day of your life and the last ones of ours. However many years that takes— but surely your lifetime—may well turn out to be the branching point between calamity and wisdom.

Did you know that your birth year—2015—was decisive? In several ways.

It was the warmest on record to that point. In the United States in the first days of December alone, 1,426 high-temperature records were broken, when you were ten months old. That was hardly a shocker since the year before was the hottest until then. And the five hottest years have been the last five years, from the year before your birth on through your 2019 birthday. In May of 2015, when you were but three months, carbon dioxide (CO_2) exceeded four hundred parts per million (ppm) for the first time in all of human history. Half that climb came after 1980, in only half my lifetime. The present 412 ppm is the highest carbon concentration in three million years! Even more alarming, its rate of increase is unprecedented in both the historical *and* geological record.

The planet's rising temperature means we're losing ice: The rate of Antarctic ice loss has tripled between 2007 and 2015.

Greenland, the second-largest ice sheet on our planet, is also melting at record rates. Dramatic sea level rise is baked in; all that melted ice has to go somewhere.

Still, the most significant news of your birth year was hardly reported at all—a new geological epoch. For the first time, the planet moved 1°C (1.7°F) above preindustrial levels and the same degree above what would have been its natural temperature. We left the Holocene for the Anthropocene. None of us was paying attention, but a geological shift was happening as your mom gave birth.

History-making response happened in 2015 as well. On December 12, 195 nations signed the Paris Agreement on climate change—a political miracle even when everyone present agreed it was only the first step. To stave off a runaway catastrophe, greenhouse gas emissions must drop to zero by 2050, when you are thirty-five.

Since your birth, we've experienced monster storms—Hurricanes Harvey, Irma, Maria, and José—and wildfires in both northern and southern California. In Barrow, Alaska, the climate-monitoring station's algorithms found the warming data so unreal they simply cleaned the slate, like your Etch-a-Sketch pad. Without algorithms for a "normal" that far out of range, the temps just disappeared from the computer record.

I fear our Holocene ways are similar. Most of us in effect clean the slate and carry on as before. We look with alarm at climate system change and then look away. In the only place it counts—our habits—we are climate-change deniers, neither ready to do anything about it nor truly to live with it.

Another 2015 response came earlier, in June—the papal encyclical, *Laudato Si'.* It's the single most powerful indictment to date of the modern world gone wrong. Moreover, it challenges what Paris still enshrines: continuing economic growth within the framework of global corporate capitalism. The encyclical speaks of climate-change impacts as "catastrophe" and "disaster," while the Paris accord uses the tepid language of "adverse effects." And the pope dares to say what Paris does not: that the happiness of the rich is subsidized by the suffering of the poor and the Earth together. Happiness comes with the debt that privilege exacts day by day from womb to tomb.

As if adding an exclamation point to the papal plea, seventeen leading climate scientists said that 2015 was the decisive moment. The window for a rise less than 2°C (3.6°F) was barely open. In a word, it was a last chance for the future we desire. Scientists rarely talked like that until now.

The third turning point all but mentioned you by name. It's *Juliana et al. v. the United States.* Twenty-one children and young adults, backed by Our Children's Trust, brought suit against the US government. The children's lawsuit argues that the government holds resources such as land and water in trust for its citizens and should be considered a trustee of the atmosphere as well. How "Kids vs. Climate" turns out, you will know. It found its prophet in Swedish climate activist Greta Thunberg and the blazing rally of four million youths in the Global Climate Strike.

However it turns out, I'm clear about another development, an awakening of sorts. We have become aware of the wonder we are. We're part of the journey of the universe! This is both sound science, Eduardo, and your identity. Your origins are stellar. The calcium in your teeth, the iron in your blood, and the gold of a wedding band you might someday wear are all gifts of exploding stars (supernovas). Indeed, every one of the ninety-four natural elements found on Earth was created in the cores of distant stars and then blasted into space, where gravity assembled them into galaxies and solar systems.

Did you know that the grace of star death funded your life and that you were starstuff before you were earthstuff? It literally takes a universe to raise a child—you, the little brother you tell us is swimming in your mommy's tummy, and all your friends, ancestors, pet turtles, and progeny.

The Crow nation knew this: "We love the stars and the stars love us back." That's the way to sing the song of life.

What I most want for you and your baby brother is that you let yourselves be overwhelmed by wonder and lose yourselves in the "kaleidoscope of creation"—not to escape this harsh world but to better inhabit it. Wondering is a way of experiencing truth. Of course, you should follow science fiercely. Tested expertise is indispensable. Yet rational analysis can miss the most essential things of life, which are bonds of love and belonging. And they are most at home in the wonder and awe that lead to knowing deeper and caring more.

Wonder sometimes comes in wee packets. I've loved watching you plant tiny carrot seeds and then seeing your delight in the first green pushing through. A carrot grows in Brooklyn.

Am I making too much of your seedlings to claim that wonder is the goal of all philosophy and theology? I doubt it, yet to date this cosmic wonder is without translation into law or even conventional consciousness. My prayer is that the children's lawsuit, together with the papal encyclical, might join the cosmology of wonder and its intergenerational ethic.

My dear child, I must break off for today, though not before a confession. It turns out that Grandma Nyla, I, and our ancestors lived our whole lives by a single fatal premise. We assumed "that what was good for us would be good for the world," as Wendell Berry put it. We were wrong.

For the rest of my days, I will puzzle how it came to pass on our watch that the Holocene morphed into the Anthropocene and we left you a diminished planet. How is it that the order of creation's well-being as primary and human well-being as derivative was flipped? How is it that our imprint is now so deep and dangerous that we are not only the ark but the flood? How is it that we missed the obvious: that it's suicidal to live our lives at the expense of planetary life and that planetary life is all we have?

The fault lies with our powers, I'm pretty sure, and the myths they serve: the myth of human centrality, the myth of our separation from nature, and the myth that we control what we create so as to render history as progress. We've lived them with such ardor that we forgot they were myths. Many live them with grasping determination still. Yet none is true.

I truly did not sit down to write you a letter like this. I had in mind something lighthearted, as love letters can be. And something adventuresome, like young people opening a door at the back of the closet into a new world. Oh well; next time. I promise more joyful things and some good stories.

Grandma Nyla and I send all our love.

Te amo,

Grandpa

TENDER YEARS

July 8, 2020

Dear Spud,

Martín, before you pillow your head on your second birthday (today!) and awaken to your third trip around the sun, I have memories to share. It's good to recall my own tender years as Grandma Nyla and I write in the autumn of our lives just as you and your brother enter the spring of yours.

My entire world at your age and until high school was "the Burg"—Petersburg, Minnesota, a village of fifty hearts on the west branch of the Des Moines River. The river, utterly indifferent to borders, quietly joined the farmlands and riparian woodlands of southern Minnesota to northern Iowa, a bike ride away.

My grandpa (your great-great-grandfather) ran the Burg's general store. The store itself is vivid in my memory.

Like the general store in many a rural village, it was the one shop with everything: outside were bags of feed and sometimes bales of hay to tide farm animals over to the next harvests. Inside, stave barrels with scoops and heavy wooden lids. I was four, five, and six during the war years, when everyone came to the store with ration books to help themselves to sugar, flour, grains, and whatever else the barrels offered. My favorites were the pickle barrel and the tall, wide-mouth jar with licorice rope.

The rest of the store was groceries, meat in a deli-like case, a few clothes and school supplies, ammonia cleaners, work gloves, fishing poles and lures, bike tire tubes, overshoes, and various sundries—everything a town's sole store was supposed to stock.

It doubled as a meeting place. Because this was wartime, conversations invariably turned to word about family members in the fighting forces. My dad had enlisted in the navy. My grandma on my mother's side had a piece of white embroidery with five red stars—one for each son in the army—on the narrow strip of wall between the two big kitchen windows. When my aunt Mabel noted the piece missing, she said, "Mother, where is your patriotism? The war's not over." Grandma, never one for words, turned from the sink to her daughter and said, "My boys are home and safe." No more needed to be said.

Grandma's spare speech was typical of the Petersens. Well, the Rasmussens too. Actually, just about everybody. Kathleen Norris, interviewing folks for *Dakota: A Spiritual Biography*, found that typical Midwesterner sentences ran the gamut from one word to two. "Yep." "Nope." "Pur-dy good." "Not bad." ("Pur-dy good" and "not bad" occupied the upper echelons of praise.) These people, Norris says, think that you get only so many words in life, and when you use them all, you die.

Yet there was always chatter in Granddad's store. I grew up watching neighbors care for one another, with their wartime solidarity and sacrifice, joy and grief, all present. Even if, in typical Minnesota fashion, they were low-key and understated, like the grainy photographs of those years.

A butcher shop joined the creamery, where I later landed my first job, scrubbing milk cans for seventy-five cents an hour. The Lutheran church and the parsonage, the teacherage and the grade school where I was the only boy in my class, Shorty's Standard Oil, and a few lanes and houses were all up the hill to the north. That rounded out the Burg, except for Vern Adams's blacksmith shop.

The blacksmith is his own story. Vern wandered in other galaxies much of the time. The fact that he toggled between our reality and his own was a curiosity for us, to be sure, but mostly we loved to just watch him hammer iron into submission, with orange, yellow, red, blue, and even purple sparks flying against his gloves, apron, and the kind of drop-down visor welders use. None of the outdoor movies we watched on Tuesday nights matched Vern's bowels-of-hell forge.

Time with him could be scary, though. He always had his shotgun near at hand in case aliens showed up without giving proper notice. He yelled at us, too. "You kids go away and never come back." But we always did. Until he died, leaving a ramshackle house stuffed floor to ceiling with hoarded goods of no measurable value or meaning, except to him.

That was pretty much the Burg, except for my mother's (your great-grandmother's) mammoth garden and Poynter's gravel pit, where we could go swimming and catch frogs until sundown if we had weeded the garden and brought bath- and dishwater in from the well.

A free-range childhood and the muddy Des Moines were world enough for us. Books other than schoolbooks were not part of our lives, so I rarely fell into a beanbag in a corner to read of other kids' adventures. Rather, we grew up outdoors in all four seasons. There was nothing we couldn't do and few things we didn't try.

One time, a big tree fell along the riverbank, and someone sawed its trunk into hunks a foot and a half long. *Perfect*, we thought as we set out to create our own raft. With a couple of planks and a rope, we wedged our sturdy ship down the soft bank into the char-brown catfish water where we were never supposed to swim or wade because it was home to big snapping turtles. Our weight pushed the raft just below the water line, it seems, so to any onlookers we were five boys walking on water. Our Sunday school teacher, Mrs. Haugland, said Jesus had done that for sure. But he was only one. We were five. And when his friend Peter tried, he panicked and sank. We neither panicked nor sank. So far as I know, we still hold the record for boys walking on water.

My most vivid memory, however, was when A. J. and Hannah Anderson told us stories. The Burg's elders, they seemed to us as old as the Ancient of Days and looked it. Both had crow's feet around wizened blue eyes that shared a twinkle and great shocks of white hair that was years beyond our grandparents' gray. Maybe they were older than the moon.

A. J. and Hannah loved telling tales of their youth, and we loved hearing them, so whenever we saw their feeble frames tending the flowers or picking apples, we made our way across the lawn in hopes of a story. People live by stories, Spud. The heart is raised on them, and we bounce off them for meaning as they knit us into bigger worlds. Sometimes only stories and compassion hold us together.

One story sticks. Something happened when A. J. was about the age we boys were then or your brother is now. He didn't remember how the news came. But the hushed report left his family sad and bewildered. The president of the United States had been assassinated on April 14, 1865, Good Friday. Shot at a theater in Washington, DC. That president was Abraham Lincoln.

Consider, then, how "old" you are today! You know someone, your grandpa, who knew someone—A. J. Anderson—who remembered Abraham Lincoln.

That's how old you are! Already in your third year, threads trail back a couple centuries. They are akin to "the mystic chords of memory" that Lincoln raised to song in his First Inaugural Address on March 4, 1861, confident they would "swell the chorus of the Union, when . . . touched . . . by the better angels of our nature."

That appeal "to the better angels of our nature" fell near the front edge of the war A. J. remembered: the Civil War. It began April 12, 1861. Better angels did not prevail.

And your great-great-grandparents on my mom's side? Their big square house with the full front porch and nine kids a couple miles from the Burg was the Petersen homestead, where I remember spring, summer, and fall days pulling weeds in the corn and beans, threshing, baling hay, milking cows, slopping pigs, soaking and plucking beheaded chickens, and picking strawberries, beans, and apples. Those 160 acres of sacred ground were the gift of the Homestead Act of 1862, signed by—you guessed it—your friend Abraham Lincoln.

And even as we had land, there were so many others, especially African Americans and Native Americans, who were effectively denied homestead. Or, for that matter, any recognition and respect. Unspoken racism was just below the surface.

THE PLANET YOU INHERIT

Well, not quite unspoken. We kids sang racist ditties about African Americans, some with the N-word, without giving the lyrics a passing thought. And we played innumerable rounds of cowboys and Indians. Cowboys never suffered a casualty, and Indians never won.

This in a community where neither African Americans nor Native Americans were ever seen. When we learned Minnesota history in the sixth grade, we were not taught that Indigenous nations were still living in "our" Minnesota, despite thousands of Indian names of counties, towns, lakes, and the state itself. (*Minnesota* is Dakota for "where the water is so clear it reflects the sky.") Nor do I recall learning that the largest public lynching in all of American history took place ninety miles from Petersburg, in Mankato, Minnesota, on the second day of Christmas, 1862. Thirty-eight Dakota warriors mounted the platform singing their haunting Christian hymn, "Great Spirit God."

The absence of Native Americans and African Americans from our textbooks didn't deter tidbits that created toxic stories, however. I remember talent shows too. One year, maybe more, Dad and his best friend wore Blackface in minstrel fashion and did their best at Black speech, jokes, and a jig to the songs of Al Jolson. "Mammy, how I love ya, how I love ya, my dear ol' mammy..."

And Dad and Loren were as kind and considerate as any men you'd meet. Which is to say that good people are sometimes captive to terrible ideas. One of evil's charming guises is innocence. This innocence is the crime.

For a long while, I marveled that so little mention of non-whites and no physical presence of them could form us deeply as racist. Then it hit me, the kind of realization that comes with a smack of the palm to the forehead. Everything and everyone was white all the time—everyone we saw and knew; the history we studied at school; all our heroes; the tales of hard work and valor on the part of our families and ancestors; our favorite stories, songs, movies, magazines, and TV shows; our teachers and pastors; and every one of our aunts, uncles, and cousins. We didn't talk about whiteness because we didn't think about it. We didn't talk about the air we breathed, either. Petersburg whiteness matched Petersburg air.

I shouldn't be surprised that whiteness bore deep into us. None of us is born conscious of the systems we enter, whether systems of oppression or routine goodness. Birth does not bring critical awareness. Birth brings only "the way things are," and we soak that up like loam does rainfall.

A cartoon on my office door has two little fish swimming together when a big fish greets them: "Good day, kids! How's the water?" As he goes on his way, one little fish says to the other, "What's water?" That was the world to us Burg fingerlings, oblivious to the water we swam in.

That milieu gave us the white gaze. White was not only "normal" for us; it was "normative" as well—the way things should be. So our white-centered perspectives became our frame of reference for understanding others and our white values the values for judging them. This cut any cords of empathy and solidarity with Black, brown, Native, and Asian Americans since we didn't need to know their stories and become part of their cultures. They needed to become part of ours. White is right; follow us. That was the norm we learned in the Burg.

Now, when I hear the phrase "people of color," as I often do, I cringe. My childhood fast-forwards into the present. To my childhood eyes, all except whites have "color." We will not be rid of racism until white is a color, too, rather than the supposedly clear lens through which white people of color view others. That others are "people of color," but not white people, is the white gaze of my childhood at work.

At the moment, I think of you and John Asante. You're only four days from being identical two-year-olds. He was born on the fourth of July, you on the eighth. Yet because he is African American, his mom will have to sit him down every so often to have "the Talk." "The Talk" is about how a young Black man survives in a racist nation where the streets are not safe if your color is not white. Your mom is spared talking to you about discrimination and survival.

Well, I've added lots about learning white racism that I didn't plan to mention as part of my tender years. And wouldn't have, had there not been a side of Petersburg that slipped my youth and I thought about only later, in college and beyond.

In any event, I send all my love as I imagine you reading this many years from now. It would be wonderful to know your response as you set your childhood alongside mine and think about how it played out. That's unlikely. But maybe I'll still have a few years, and I can sit in a rickety chair like A. J. and tell you stories.

Te amo,

Grandpa

SOMETHING TO WRITE HOME ABOUT

July 15, 2020

Dear Spud,

When your dad was seven, we were on sabbatical in Arusha, Tanzania. A safari from Arusha to the edge of the Serengeti took us to Olduvai Gorge, renowned as the place where *Homo habilis* ("skillful human") was first unearthed in 1964. This was a line of hominins using stone tools dating from 2.35 to 1.5 million years ago, long before the anatomically "modern" human line that we are (*Homo sapiens sapiens*). Researchers Louis and Mary Leakey sent their findings about human origins from Olduvai Gorge into people's living rooms all around the world via television.

What most interested your dad were Olduvai's massive, mythical creatures. Like a saber-toothed tiger the size of a horse, a giant sloth of similar measure, and a bison-like beast double that bulk. Yet what snagged my attention were the precursors to you, me, and all other modern humans. The oldest footprints found to date—3.6 million years old—were discovered at Laetoli, not far from where we were camping. On a work break, Mary Leakey's high-spirited staff started throwing dried chunks of elephant dung at each other. One of the workers, ducking and falling onto all fours, found himself staring at those footprints.

We didn't see any footprints or ancient hominid bones, but I do remember a staff member's story about an ancient human line at Olduvai. In the corner of the tent that shaded his dig from the equatorial sun rested a partial farm plot that was irrigated with channels that sent water in different directions. Through soil dating and artifacts, the researchers learned that the plot reached back to the beginnings of agriculture twelve thousand years ago, when the late Holocene began. Yet that method of irrigation was, he told us, one the elders of his village knew from their ancestors.

Is this possible? A layer at Olduvai with human practices that, over millennia, were never forgotten? Is it possible that human habits have that kind of staying power even as time tries to expunge the past?

That hot afternoon at Olduvai shed light on a big question humans have always asked: Where did we come from, and how did we get here? And it raised an even bigger one: What does it mean to be a human being? Who are we in the grand scheme of things? And are we the same now as we've always been or different? These puzzles surface again as I think about the world you're toddling into.

Where *have* we come from, and how *did* we get here? Your brother just finished a timeline. It begins right where it should, with single-celled creatures. Then come the dinosaurs, next the mammals, and finally the Romans and the Vikings. I'm not sure why he finished with the Vikings. Because they were all Rasmussens? I'll ask.

But Eduardo's sketch needs an addition or two. Luckily, help is on the way from Louise Leakey, of the third generation of the fabled family. She uses an image every toddler knows well: it's the toilet paper you unspool like a pro. No matter how many times you've done it, you still giggle as tissue falls atop your bare feet.

There are four hundred sheets of tissue in the roll Leakey uses to tell Earth time. As an experiment, lay out the roll down the hallway, into your room, and back several times over. Then count the sheets starting from the first one. You need to go from sheet 1 to about sheet 100, around 3.8 billion years ago, before first life appears. These founding members are single-celled organisms called *prokaryotes*. They were around a very long time (and are still dominant) before multicelled organisms evolved called *eukaryotes*, the kind of cells you and I have. Geologists call that monotonous stretch of single-cell years "the boring billion," so jump ahead to all those dinosaurs your brother knows by heart. They come eons later, at sheet 381. That's nineteen *before the end*, nineteen before your birthday and Eduardo's.

Dinosaurs lived much longer than humans have to date, making it all the way to sheet 395, five before the end. That's 170 million years! Their death sixty-six million years ago ended the Age of Reptiles and opened the door for the Age of Mammals. It happened quickly and catastrophically, thanks to a colossal asteroid crashing in the Yucatán about the same time as huge volcanic eruptions upended portions of the Indian subcontinent. Because of all the debris layered into the atmosphere, there were a couple years of darkened skies and mass extinction followed.

Aren't you grateful that the sequence was as Eduardo has it, with the Age of Mammals *after* the Age of Reptiles? Had it been the other way around, we'd not have known each other and laughed together, read stories, or played hide and seek. No birthday parties, either, or soft-serve coconut yogurt down on Fifth Avenue.

Yet our story as human mammals doesn't begin when the dinosaurs end. It begins on the final half sheet, sheet four hundred. Our distant ancestors emerge there among sixteen different lines of upright apes. You, Grandma Nyla, and everyone you have ever heard about belong to the last surviving line of those sweet sixteen. Taxonomist Carl Linnaeus named us *Homo sapiens sapiens*—the Wise Ape. I'm not so sure we're wise. Richard Leakey, Louise's father, says we're the only species he knows that is capable of making consistently bad choices!

We started marking time thirty thousand generations ago, roughly two hundred thousand years but maybe longer. Of the upright apes we know about, numerous lines lived at the same time, if not always in the same space. We had mixed-marriage children with one of them, the Neanderthals, and maybe a second, the Denisovans. It's also possible that *Homo denisovan* was the ancestor to both *Homo sapiens* and *Homo neanderthalensis.*

Keep the yard light on for other relatives dropping by—new discoveries are being made all the time. *Homo longi* was recently unearthed at a construction site in China and given the nickname Dragon Man, from the Dragon River region where *longi* lived. The oldest of our kind, *Homo sapiens,* were around then, as were *Homo naledi* in South Africa, *Homo floresiensis* in Indonesia, and *Homo luzonensis* in the Philippines. Lots of different human tribes side by side.

I haven't had my DNA swabbed yet, but I'll wear it as a badge of honor if I have Neanderthal or, even better, Dragon Man genes. Many *sapiens* have leftovers.

We *Homo sapiens* are all African by origin. That's the short answer to where we came from.

Carl Anthony, an architect and activist, was in Nairobi shortly after Barack Obama was elected president. Anthony commented to his taxi driver, "You must be very proud that a US president has a Kenyan father and is half African." To which the driver replied, "Sir, all the US presidents are African. They all came from here."

Some of our people stayed in Africa, but many left. Starting about seventy-five thousand years ago, and one step at a time, they populated much of the planet's hospitable land, with *Homo sapiens* eventually the only surviving hominin species.

But *Homo sapiens* living alone on the planet is an exception. The historical norm is multiple human species abreast of one another. Will that happen again? Evolution's full of surprises—actually, it counts on them—so it's possible.

But right now it's just us. And where are we on your toilet roll? *Homo sapiens'* years are the last two millimeters of the last sheet. That's 0.0787 inches of precious toilet paper. In that slender space, your lifetime and mine is too thin a sliver even to draw with a thick Magic Marker. We are but a blip in Earth time; in space, a scratch.

How long will we be around? We don't know. We do know that every species dies. None is immortal. I personally hope we match the dinosaurs' tally. Fourteen and a half sheets is a very good run, though even that doesn't look promising since we are currently driving Earth's sixth mass extinction.

Mass extinctions are very rare. We've had only five such extinctions since multicellular organisms appeared 600 million years ago. Extinctions don't make "mass" until death is dealt to 70 percent or more of existing species, with each extinction moving through life like a machete. And while each also opens pathways to a different expression of life, the new community normally takes millions of years to come of age. Some species survive mass extinction, but the planet never dials back to the life community it knew.

There is no dialing back. The harsh truth is that we are now creating extinction across the very community upon which we depend utterly. We're running Genesis backward. It's frightfully simple: When nature's history is our own, ecocide is fratricide. We're here, it's wonderful, we're gorgeous . . . and then we're gone, all under our own power. How ironic it would be if *sapiens,* the reasoning, clever ape, brought the last human line to its end while still in its youth.

I don't want to scare the bejesus out of you. Oddly, there's solace in the fact that the future always wears a veil. It's only when a trend's run its course that it is fully revealed.

Whatever Earth's present course, our death-dealing likely won't be the worst. That was the Great Dying, 252 million years ago. At that time, 96 percent of early forests, almost all herbivores plus marine species, sloughed off their mortal coil. A different community came only in the course of tens of millions of years. Rehab takes forever.

We are, in any case, only at the onset of the mass extinction for which we are uniquely responsible. There is still time to avert the worst. The bracing reality is that we are extinguishing species of mammals, reptiles, birds, insects, plants, and microbes at a *rate* faster than previous extinctions, with the exception of that alien asteroid. So while the *numbers* ploughed under for good do not yet make "mass extinction," the *speed* portends catastrophe. We are the apocalypse.

And extinction is only a corner of the horror. Diminished populations, stopping short of eternal death and still surviving, may hold even greater change for you. What happens if 75 percent of insect populations die and we lose our pollinators? What happens when the marine life nurseries—coral reefs—bleach and die? (We've lost 30 percent so far.) Or when fish, a major source of protein, are unavailable or unaffordable? Species populations of fish have halved since 1970, when I was thirty-one. Although most species hold on and don't go extinct, their diminished numbers leave the web of life in tatters.

So amid all this drama in your world, how old are you? Louise Leakey has been hunting fossils since she was twelve. But now, and unlike her grandparents, she and her colleagues extract DNA to fill out the story of our origins. And you know what? DNA, the life code written in every cell of every creature, shows that we're related to all creatures, including plants and fungi. And here's a stunner. You and I have mitochondria, the organelles that orchestrate energy production in cells. They're inherited from our mothers, and that maternal transmission can be traced back to a single woman living 150 to 200 thousand years ago! So thanks to your mom, you're the offspring of a kind of Eve. And that's not a metaphor.

Here's a fun aside. Nyla and I were in Cambridge, England, for a short teaching gig. We went to the Eagle Pub and saw the corner table where James Watson and Francis Crick imbibed regularly and where they announced to the world that they had discovered the double helix of DNA. We followed their example, at least the part that hoists a pint in celebration. Our choice? An IPA called Eagle DNA. Pubs are great places to learn about life.

There's still more. Today's *Santa Fe New Mexican* carries a report tucked into the last page. It's about "the oldest stuff on Earth," seven-billion-year-old stardust. That "stuff" is microscopic grains of a meteorite that landed in Australia. The grains are about half as old as the universe itself, thus older than our solar system. These stardust grains, taking shape like granola clusters, were part of the debris that formed our planet. Your body, too, carries these gifts of stars that went wild and, with such meteors, showered immortality everywhere. In that those seven-billion-year-old meteor grains are now also earthdust and so are you, you're older than Earth itself, by a long shot.

So we've answered our questions of where we came from, how we got here, and how old you are on your second birthday. I also want to say that you're alive at the most important time *for* life on the beleaguered planet you inherit. Don't give up on home! Earth is full of genius and generates life in wild ways. "In nature improbabilities are the one stock in trade," Annie Dillard says, "the whole creation is one lunatic fringe."

More in the next letter. Love from Grandma too. Feel our hugs.

Te amo,

Grandpa

YOU FINISH
THE STORY

Dear Martín,

Will you respond differently to your world than Grandma Nyla and I do? She and I have seen the first impacts of the climate crisis, but you and Eduardo will be living Earth's fever throughout your lives. Will you behave differently than we did? I think so. Because you enter at the onset of a new life, not at the end of an old one.

I've read stories of "the American Serengeti," the Great Plains, when they teemed with bison and deer, antelope and elk, wolves and coyotes, innumerable black bears, and even grassland grizzlies. There were songbird melodies by the flock and rivers and lakes so plentiful with fish they could be caught with a simple net. And while that paints a vision of wondrous plenitude, I've never felt the loss of worlds I never knew. Atlantis is gone, but I don't miss it. And you do not miss Petersburg.

So does loss matter? You may find Brooklyn magical and sufficient and never miss, say, the absent glaciers of Glacier National Park. It scares me how easily we adapt to deprivation, but it's probably essential to survival. You can live without feeling the loss I experience as a burden or an ache.

Still, there's the imprinting of childhood. I continue to glean meanings I soaked up like a sponge in my tender years. Robin Wall Kimmerer's Evon Peter, a Gwich'in man of northeastern Alaska, jumps to mind. Evon says he "was raised by the river." Not *near* the river, *by* the river. The river formed who he was, what his community was, and how he belonged. Me too.

In any case, as an Anthropocene kid, you belong in a new Earth world. And while this world was given to you by others and isn't one you created, it's nonetheless brand new to you. The future, then, may feel open to you, not foreboding and closed as it feels to me and Grandma Nyla many a day. You may not feel the eco-lament we do either, at least not as a burden you've been responsible for.

On the other hand, you may, like us, be convinced that planetary suffering is unjust, unacceptable, and unnecessary. You may also promise to alleviate it, as we have. Perhaps that will strike you as the once-in-a-lifetime opportunity to which you'll commit your life's work.

You may even befriend the world we leave you. *Sapiens* are wonderfully adept. The world moves around us in ways grand and small, and we change shape to fit in. When I think back on my own childhood and youth, the world never seemed fallen, despite what we learned in catechism class. Or maybe we just got used to the Fall and made our way from there. Enjoyed it too.

I think of human beings traversing millennia. Most lived lives ranging from hard to terrible. Yet they loved, danced, celebrated, feasted, and bore their children in hope and promise. Hard times didn't preclude meaningful lives, even joyous ones.

Here's the point: Humans are endlessly resilient, creative, and adaptive. That is the stuff of our better angels. So is our resistance to injustice and oppression. I once interviewed surviving members of the resistance against Hitler, people who had plotted to end the Third Reich. I often came away shaking my head in disbelief. But not only because of the extraordinary risks they took and the courage I could not imagine for myself. Rather, that somehow those terrible years added up to what, judging from their animated retelling, seemed essential to who they were and how they faced life. The theologian Dietrich Bonhoeffer, among the victims of the Third Reich, said he would not have wished to live in another time, despite the fact that "we cannot even plan for the next day [and] that what we have built up is being destroyed overnight."

Almost by accident I came upon Viktor Frankl's *Man's Search for Meaning*, an account of his Holocaust experiences. I could only conclude that for him those terrible years were, somehow or other, filled with meaning. *Meaning* and a *why* for lives of danger carried prisoners up one mountain and down and then up the next. A robust *why* bolstered the innate will to survive.

Although the cruel forge may be hardship and suffering, sometimes amid it human beings arrive where Frankl did. He wrote friends very shortly after he was liberated from the concentration camp:

> I am unspeakably tired, unspeakably sad, unspeakably lonely. . . . In the camp, you really believed you had reached the low point of life—and then, when you came back, you were forced to see that things had

not lasted, everything that had sustained you had been destroyed, that at the same time when you had become human again, you could sink even deeper into an even more bottomless suffering. Maybe there is nothing else left but to weep a little and to search through the Psalms. Maybe you will laugh at me, maybe you will be angry with me; but I do not contradict myself in the least; I take back nothing of my old affirmation of life when I experience the things I have described. On the contrary: if I had not had this rock-solid positive attitude to life, what would have become of me during these weeks, indeed those months in the concentration camp? But I see things in another dimension now. Increasingly, I realize that life is so infinitely meaningful that even in suffering and even in failure there still has to be a meaning.

What Grandma Nyla and I wish for you is "this rock-solid positive attitude to life," that even in suffering there still has to be meaning. If you find your way in life, it will be because of the meaning you found, and the meaning you gave, as you and your generation face down the single greatest collective challenge humankind has ever confronted.

Humans have long degraded their environments, sometimes to the point of exhaustion of their own living worlds or, more likely, the worlds of those they conquered and colonized. But if the stark warnings of the IPCC and the UN are as well founded as daily apocalypse reports and California fires now make obvious, then my ancestors and I have done something qualitatively different than what we had in the Holocene. Australia is aflame as I write. An area the size of Switzerland is charred and littered with millions of dead animals. The "trees of ashes wave goodbye to goodbye" as ecologists become coroners. And as I mentioned in a previous letter, the melt rate of Antarctic ice has tripled in a decade, threatening dramatically higher seas sooner rather than later.

I don't mean only that we've ravaged the natural world in the process of thinking we could build our way out of nature into a habitat of our own (the myth of separation). I mean we have reengineered nature as a whole such that Earth has been set on a new course. Something like an "evolutionary reset" is the astonishing circumstance that falls to you and yours. That's Anthropocene singularity.

Your vocation, your calling, your Great Work will be to remap the world on an altered Earth for a different way of life in an uncharted future. The relatively stable center of the Holocene no longer holds. You, then, are setting out on a new age of discovery and a dangerous pilgrimage. Yet you may find the meaning of that journey strangely life giving! You may find in it the *why* that will not let you go even as you live into the unknown. You may even find unlimited enthusiasm for unprecedented challenges. I suspect you will find yourself "saying yes to life in spite of everything."

I think of Greta Thunberg, the environmental activist. You've likely heard about her, perhaps from her. At sixteen she began the school strikes for climate action that became a movement of world youth. This thrust her onto the world stage, where, like a prophet, she has been unrelenting about a brave commitment for urgent action to confront climate calamity. Since her campaign always bore bad news about a worsening reality—a stark planetary emergency is upon us, she repeated over and over—people thought she herself must suffer its message. Her response? "People seem to think I am depressed, or angry, or worried, but that's not true. It was like I got meaning in my life." Leading the charge in a great cause is exhilarating and gives her satisfaction and meaning.

Still, I worry about the burden you and Eduardo will carry and how it will affect you. The Talmud is wise about this: "You are not obligated to complete the task. But neither are you free to desist from it." Your calling is to take a few steps for a new chapter, not put the old world back together or finish the new one.

Just begin.

I so hope you and Eduardo make this adventure your life. It's not often that the chance to create civilization comes calling.

Perhaps surprisingly, this new journey will find you disinterring the oldest questions. For you the big-idea questions will be existential. You will answer them for a different time, place, and planet, with stakes higher than my generation ever knew.

All that is for other letters, however. Until then, dear child, all my love. Grandma Nyla's too. We squeeze you tight across the miles.

Abrazos!

Grandpa

LOVE IN A TIME OF PLAGUE

April 22, 2020

Dear Eduardo,

Life goes on—six feet apart.

You and Martín are stuck at home. Your parents too. We all are, across the country and around the world. A tiny microbe highjacked us. We don't even see our captors.

How could we? Ten trillion coronaviruses weigh less than a single raindrop! Maybe they look like teeny tadpoles or starbursts, perhaps the tiniest galaxy ever. I imagine wiggly worms tangled in knots.

But we need not imagine. Good microscopes expose them. They're plump with lots of little crowns—thus, "corona" (*crown*) virus. Those little crowns are spiky proteins that latch like Velcro onto cells in our respiratory system. They swarm and then burrow to commandeer our breathing.

How fitting that they wear a symbol of royal rule, their "corona," and bring proud humans to their knees without so much as a scepter. It's mob rule by gazillions of unseen microbes, a ridiculous version of the meek inheriting the Earth.

Viruses get a bad rap, though I'm certain the coronavirus deserves it. *Virus* is Latin for "poison." Yet 8 percent of the human genome is genes implanted by viruses we'd be dead without. Actually, we wouldn't *be* at all since select viruses let the placenta develop and thus the baby. We wouldn't be here at all, either, without viruses aiding photosynthesis. The air we breathe is, in part, courtesy of viruses. Credit belongs where due.

I don't mean to divert our attention or make light of the pandemic. Our internal clocks wobble, and normalcy's circadian rhythms have been blasted to smithereens. I find myself checking the calendar for the day of the week, even the month, only to stare at blank whitespace where reminders usually competed for space.

Frankly, it's lonely. Yes, Nyla and I do see friends, and we did go to church several times in Holy Week. But only "virtually," which means "not really."

Then there's the coronacoaster—the pandemic ups and downs. As one Facebook meme put it, "One day you're loving your bubble, doing workouts, baking banana bread, and going for long walks. The next day you're crying, drinking gin for breakfast, and missing people you don't even like." Weariness and depression crouch just around the corner, and if we can't make good cheer together, they weasel in and weigh us down. Humor is Gilead's balm. Martin Luther, writing as the bubonic plague nipped at Wittenberg, had it right: "You have as much faith as you have laughter. If there's no laughter in heaven, I don't want to go there." Me either.

Yet despite the lightheartedness, this experience worms its way into our psyches. We're not meant to be literally out of touch. We're social creatures; we're party animals; we're huggers.

Eduardo, you will likely remember this off-balance world like I remember World War II. Right now, every home is the front line, however. Where you live in New York, there aren't the usual crowds, the frenetic pace, the cacophony—just eerie silence. Eerily silent, that is, except for wailing ambulances and police sirens. It's fifteen thousand deaths and counting in your city and state as of today, Earth Day, and fifty thousand across the United States. Soon, virus deaths will surpass twenty years of fighting in another war, Vietnam.

This is scary, and Nyla and I are genuinely frightened. It's always reassuring to see you every weekend, thanks to Face-Time. Meanwhile, empty streets and crowded hospitals must make the city feel like one big waiting room.

Maybe you won't remember. The worst plague in modern times, just a century ago, is hardly noted. That plague killed fifty million people in three years and changed the world forever. But try to find a brass plaque or monuments in graveyards. Instead, people memorialize the "war to end all wars" that didn't—World War I. (When did waging war ever end wars?) The 1918 influenza epidemic killed more than twice as many people as WWI, with which it overlapped. Yet few remember. If there are no memorials and few stories, maybe you won't remember COVID-19 either.

The reason I write of love in a time of plague is my crescendo-ing sense of what is most dear. Threats to what Nyla and I want to protect with every fiber of our being put us in a mood to say "I love you" to most everything—azure New Mexico skies, the birds splashing in the birdbath and singing in the piñons, the serenity of this neighborhood, a wave from a neighbor. We even want to say "I love you" to every grain of sand in the arroyo and the rain splattering the sand right now.

I also write because I don't know what other than *love* describes those who put themselves in harm's way day in and day out for us. Nurses, doctors, ambulance drivers, the EMT squad; police and firefighters; custodians and cleaning personnel; those stocking grocery shelves and working the checkout lanes; people packing food bags for families whose money is gone; the folks leaning into cars at drive-thru testing stations; mail carriers and meatpackers; farm workers; the up-close aides in nursing homes.

They're essential workers, "essential" as in our lives depend upon them.

We can get along quite well without hedge fund owners, corporate lawyers, and Wall Street odds-makers. We cannot get along without the salt-of-the-earth workers, millions of them immigrants who toil in demeaning, health-threatening conditions. They are paid poorly, have few if any benefits, live in crowded housing, and are accorded little or no respect. And they are among the first to contract COVID-19.

So I must talk of love. Of course, talk *of* love, or *about* love, is feeble compared to the real thing—loving and being loved. Love's meaning blossoms only when it's embodied; only when, like the courage and sacrifice of those essential workers, it goes public. Love unembodied is mute; alive, it's more verb than noun.

Love as a verb is normally busy, a continuous apprenticeship where we're always learning in person. Let's just be aware that while ideas always matter, in the end what matters most are not good ideas, even good ideas about love, but good communities, formed by love.

It's something as simple as our church fund that pays a local tacos place and a little restaurant to stay open and deliver one hundred meals a day to homeless shelters. At least this keeps a few people at work and offers a dusting of love to the displaced. Charity, I know, is only a stopgap. Yet for now we need high-volume charity on the way to big changes and justice.

Do you remember that at 7:00 p.m. on some nights in your neighborhood people started leaning out of the windows, standing in doorways, stepping onto balconies, even climbing to rooftops to bang pans, ring bells, clang make-do cymbals, and howl their thanks to the frontline heroes who had spent yet another day attending the sick and dying? You, Martín, and your parents stepped out on the deck to stand on the big table your dad made and add your voices to the noise of gratitude.

That ritual spread a bit of love.

But what is love? What can we say about love that holds for all its forms and nuances, long after this particular plague is over?

We know what love feels like. It's the flush of excitement at a child's first steps or the screech of a toddler who finds a Cheerio between the couch cushions. It's the pride of every parent and teacher as children sound out their first words in their first book. It's the quiet routines of a good marriage. It's friendship, giddiness, romance and what it leads to. It's intimate, passionate, and empathic.

All these are love as belonging, belonging to and with others, being with them and for them. Maybe *belonging* is love's best synonym.

Not every belonging is love, though. Love is belonging with equal care and equal regard, the kind of love that puts another's life in the same framework and on the same terms as one's own. No difference in the fare, as Josiah Young says—that's Golden

Rule love, "love-neighbor-as-self" love. (I personally like Wendell Berry's version: "Do unto those downstream from you as you would have those upstream do unto you.")

My latest all-time favorite book is Robin Wall Kimmerer's *Braiding Sweetgrass.* In the chapter "Epiphany in the Beans," Kimmerer is teaching her daughters to garden. Gardening is about "ultimate reciprocity," Kimmerer's words for loving and being loved in return. The epiphany, courtesy of the beans, is that land responds to caring gardeners and loves them back: "She loves us with beans and tomatoes, with roasting ears and blackberries and birdsongs. By a shower of gifts and a heavy rain of lessons. She provides for us and teaches us to provide for ourselves. That's what good mothers do." Later, Kimmerer says she's grateful her girls learned to garden because their gardens will be good mothers to them when she is gone. This is an apt description of love, which she says is about nurturing well-being, sharing resources, working together for the common good, and creating beauty. It is, she says, "a celebration of shared values."

Love has that kind of embrace; it's inclusive in that way. It extends to various entities—some of which are like us, while many are not; some of which are human, while many are other-than-human. On its best days it even puts enemies in the same moral framework with us. It builds community.

Most of the time, love is happiness. But sometimes it's heartbreak, as it is with stage-four cancer, a tragic accident, a suicide, or the onset of Alzheimer's. What do we say about love, and what does love say when tragedy crashes into our safe, serene spaces?

My brother died by suicide at age forty-nine. If anyone had thought to say to Mom that the devastating grief Bruce's suicide caused was too great a price to pay for loving him, she would only have stared in disbelief.

The choice is not whether to love in the face of suffering. It's only how to lament love's loss when the tears won't stop and there is "no sorrow like my sorrow," as the Bible says. Where to go, whom to befriend, and what to do when what is most precious is gone forever—these are the choices. Not whether to love.

Don't let me scare you off, Eduardo. The last thing I want is to warn you against a life of love because it can hurt and wound. Passion and commitment *do* exact their price, and often it's high. To love, then, is to risk a lot: loss, anguish, grief, heartbreak. And the most intense suffering is matched to our deepest loves. To avoid suffering, then, the logical thing is to avoid loving.

Yet nobody does. Something soul-deep kicks in to risk love over and over again. My mom—your great-grandma—might even have told you, as she tried to cope with Bruce's suicide, that never to love means never to live.

It's late, and I must close. But there's one more thing: Love is always more. If you love more, you risk more. If you love more, you worry more. If you love more, you hope more. If you love more, you sing more.

Grandma Nyla and I send hugs and imagine a goodnight story or two. Think good thoughts, bang a cymbal at 7:00 p.m., and keep us in your dreams. We'll do the same for you.

Te amo,

Grandpa

"LOVE WITH LEGS"

June 8, 2020

Dear Eduardo,

While it's quite easy to live and love when all is well, how do we live and love if ours is a dying world and a broken society? What manner of love takes the measure of emergencies as standard fare?

Run with this: we're seeking "love with legs." *Love with legs* is how Cornel West describes justice. Justice is love gone public and systemic.

There's another name for it—prophetic love. From the Hebrew prophets all the way to the present, prophets are interpreters of history. It's their job to evoke a love-and-justice purpose and see it through as if life depended upon it. Drunk with God's pathos, prophets are less interested in seeing what we know than in understanding what we see. The gravity of stark facts in plain sight is their obsession.

The result is double edged. First they give us a laser-like message on the past as that past punches into the present. Then they offer the vision of a different future. Both are for such a time as this.

Imagine you're hosting a dinner party, Eduardo. You'd invite a few prophets to enjoy crusty bread, good wine, and conversation about love. You might invite Amos and Isaiah to be "then" and Greta Thunberg and Pope Francis to be "now."

It might be awkward at times. Prophets wail an octave higher and shriller than we find comfortable. That's intentional. They mean to raise the decibels of the anguished to a pitch the complacent can't help but hear.

Eduardo, on your street, a few doors toward Sixth Avenue, is a double-windowed doorway. In one window is a sign, "White supremacy is oppression." In the other, "Love knows no borders," written in Arabic, Spanish, and English. That's prophetic speech—utterly spare, cutting, and pointed. White supremacy excludes; love embraces.

Right now, with Earth hurtling toward apocalypse, we need prophets more than ever. But how will we recognize the ones in our midst? How do we know who to listen to?

The Santa Fe writer Rabbi Nahum Ward-Lev says that in the Hebrew prophets, three themes emerge: "an encounter with divine love and concern for the world, courage to name oppression, and moral imagination to articulate an alternative future." Those three themes can help you know a prophet when you see one. By the way, how did Greta and the pope get along with Amos at your dinner party?

Prophecy's first theme—divine love and care for the world—rests in the conviction that we all live in the presence of a great love that embraces the whole world and the whole of our lives. This love covers every inner and outer journey, spans geological epochs, casts out fear, and is stronger than death. Rabbi Nahum's translation from Hebrew for the source of this love is "Living Presence."

Kosuke Koyama comes to mind when I think of this love. A colleague at Union, he had a twinkle in his eye that you would have enjoyed. Ko survived the firebombing of Tokyo in 1945. He was running for safety when a bomb screamed through the air to bury itself in front of him. A dud. Decades later, Ko said he was still trying to craft the right paragraph about that moment in his life.

After the war, Ko lived in Thailand for a while, eventually coming to New York to teach. We had a little celebration when Japan declared him a "national treasure." (The Japanese do that when elders turn sixty-five.)

Ko once wrote that,

Love has its speed. It is an inner speed. It is a spiritual speed. It is a different kind of speed from the technological speed to which we are accustomed. It is "slow" yet it is lord over all other speeds since it is the speed of love. It goes on in the depth of our life, whether we notice or not, at three miles an hour. It is the speed we walk and therefore it is the speed the love of God walks.

Ko once said there arrives a point at the depth of every religion where religion matters not at all any longer. Love alone does, at three miles an hour.

"Courage to name oppression" is the second prophetic element. Confronting injustice with courage is the way of prophetic love. It is, as my colleague Beverly Wildung Harrison used to say, the power of anger in the work of love.

As I write, outrage in Minneapolis at the brutal police murder of George Floyd, yet another unarmed Black man, has ignited protests across the country and around the world. Floyd's death comes after Breonna Taylor's, shot in her apartment by police carrying a no-knock search warrant and looking for someone else. And it comes after Ahmaud Arbery's killing by white men in south Georgia. Had there not been videos of Floyd's and Arbery's killings, their cases would have disappeared somewhere in the basement shadows of local "systems of justice."

In Minnesota, a state no one ever listed with those of the Jim Crow Deep South, Black people are *four times* as likely to be killed by the police as white people. The system has carried on, with white indifference, for decades.

Thankfully, this June, millions—Black, white, brown, Native, Asian—are demanding an end to systemic racism. The Black Lives Matter banner, now seen everywhere, insists on the shared humanity and equal value of Black lives. Fairness and equality— those classic marks of justice-love—are the presenting issues. On last night's news, a protester kept telling the reporter, "I don't preach violence. I preach equality." And the editorial-page cartoon in the paper today has a person ascending a ladder to put a missing word in place above the entrance to the US Supreme Court. The word missing is "EQUAL"; the rest of the phrase is "JUSTICE UNDER LAW," and the person climbing the ladder says, "One of these days it'll stick."

What we are seeing right now is the courage to name and call out oppression—the courage to make equality stick. That's prophetic love.

The third element—moral imagination to articulate an alternative future—is the quest for "an inclusive economic and social order in which all beings would flourish." Note that Nahum did not say "all humans"; he said "all beings."

That quest for an alternative future is palpable on this warm June day as some people use their moral imagination to summon a viable and sustainable economy, political order, and culture. With the exception of the 1960s, I do not recall a time so eager for big changes and so intent upon realizing them. Or so resistant to them. (That also mirrors the '60s.)

Your mom must have recited the Pledge of Allegiance to the Flag when she became a US citizen. There's a pledge within that pledge. It's to "liberty and justice for all," the same pledge I used to make the first thing each morning in grade school. We stood beside our desks, faced the flag next to the teacher, and put a hand over our hearts to pledge allegiance.

"Liberty and justice for all" is justice measured in the same way for everyone. It's what real prophets are always aiming for, and it's their goal for the future.

In a book I wrote, I give the name "anticipatory communities" to this quest. "Anticipatory communities are home places where it's possible to reimagine worlds and reorder possibilities" for a better way of life. You get up in the morning to practice a different future.

These societies in the making, which usually start with local communities, vary widely because they form in different places with different peoples of different cultures, traditions, and resources. Yet they share distinctive marks.

They are havens. They are separate and safe, yet eager to take on possibilities. You feel at home at the same time you feel part of a great adventure together, even when that adventure does not know where it ends or what it will meet along the way.

In these communities, formation happens by conscious choice rather than passive acceptance of the culture's unwritten ethic. For anticipatory communities, values are consciously embodied in community practices oriented to the common good. Such is "love with legs" now—love gone public, prophetic love. It's living in the presence of a world-embracing love, it's holding a moral plumb line to society to courageously reveal and name oppression, and it's seeking an alternative future by way of communities that anticipate that future even in a time of great uncertainty, perhaps *especially* in a time of great uncertainty. Prophetic love plays out as justice, fidelity to the bonds of relationship lived in mutually enhancing ways.

How does justice-love go public? When Martin Luther King Jr., speaking often of love, broke particular laws, risked jail, and pleaded for others to do the same, he wasn't only witnessing to noncompliance with evil. He was pressuring the nation to enact and enforce laws so that a racist nation wouldn't have to wait until racism was eradicated from each heart, mind, and soul before justice was done for the disenfranchised. Here are King's words: "The law can't make a man love me, but it can restrain him from lynching me. . . . So while the law may not change the hearts of men, it does change the habits of men. And when you change the habits of men, pretty soon the attitudes and the hearts will be changed."

In short, love gone public alters relationships by way of systemic behavioral changes that precede and shape attitudinal ones.

Here's a bit more about systems and people. None of us is born morally upright. Instead, self and society are twinborn and always in process together. So when you arrived in 2015, you landed in a world with elaborate moral and cultural infrastructure and institutionalized ways of meeting basic needs, whether physical, mental, or spiritual. It had its own way of life already baked in, already "systematized."

Systems-love, then, responds not in individual random acts of kindness or Hallmark sentiment. It's love as "ecological-economic vocation" and reform. Nothing random about it, nothing sentimental about it. It holds together rage, negotiation, and structural change.

Persons and systems interact reciprocally. We shape the world; the world shapes us. We create the systems; the systems create us. We construct our habitat; our habitat fashions us. Being shapes doing, and doing shapes being, never one without the other.

Systems long in place create autopilot. They so shape us, and we them, that we think and act through them. They create and channel our behavior, whether loving or unjust.

It takes prophets to help us wake up from being on autopilot, recognize the systems that are shaping us, and break the cycle.

Find the prophets, Eduardo, and listen to them. Because unless you address issues systemically, the hardship and suffering from, say, climate calamity, will be distributed as unevenly as wealth presently is. Climate caste will parallel racial and economic caste.

Let's end this with a starter list for love that we hope is tuned to meeting planetary emergencies head on, then moves into a different kind of future. That's love doing all it can to:

- systemically reduce inequality and suffering;
- compensate loss;
- protect and maximize freedom;

- pursue the common good and enhanced quality of life for all;
- achieve and sustain a safe and healthy environment;
- eschew double standards and enforce the rule of law; and
- foster truth and trust in government of, for, and by the people.

I know that reads with all the excitement of a grocery list. If lists don't inspire, here's paleontologist and priest Pierre Teilhard de Chardin for your backpack or bathroom mirror: "The day will come when, after harnessing space, the winds, the tides, and gravitation, we shall harness for God the energies of love. And on that day, for the second time in the history of the world, we will have discovered fire."

May it be so! It's the love Grandma Nyla and I send you.

Te amo,

Grandpa

THE KINDNESS OF MICROBIAL STRANGERS

June 10, 2020

Dear Eduardo,

How's your day going? Give us a call and tell us your favorite part so far. You and I were in the middle of a mini-seminar when the bell rang. But there was another question, maybe two. Such as: Now that we're in the Anthropocene epoch, does that change love? Does the rolling apocalypse make a difference?

The pandemic, climate catastrophe, and justice movements have gone global in the Anthropocene. COVID-19 has reached every corner of the planet except Antarctica. For climate rupture, even Antarctica doesn't get a pass. The planetwide impact of the virus and climate is the first meaning of going global.

Globalization, a new word in your grandparents' lifetime, has ramped this up by girdling the planet to determine the flow of food, energy, transportation, information, finance, and communication. Thus did COVID-19 take to the air in first class, business, and coach from China to the United States, South

Korea, Singapore, Europe, Russia, and India, all in a matter of days. As one disease expert put it, "a disease anywhere is a disease everywhere." Global supply lines, ferried by planes, ships, trucks, buses, and cars, make the spread of epidemics and pandemics faster and more likely. You'll face more of them on a shrinking, accelerating planet.

On a different note, but global as well, social media makes organizing faster and likelier than was thought possible a half century ago. Protests in the wake of George Floyd's death happened everywhere, simultaneously. The scene of the crime, Minneapolis, was only the portal.

I initially celebrated globalization's webs of interdependence, but I came to realize that it carries a curse. The curse is that disabling events in one part of the world—rising sea levels, drought and famine, hurricanes and floods, the migration of peoples, blocked access to critical resources, epidemics and pandemics, terrorism domestic and foreign—deliver harm to zip codes far from their origin. Ask Midwest farmers and rural towns about dependence on international markets and contentious trade policy. The traditional pastoral serenity Grandma Nyla and I knew as children is illusory.

Pandemics and climate rupture are also profound events of the natural world. The consequence is that the widening, deepening human imprint—nature is us, and we are nature—expands human responsibility and mandates new dimensions of collective accountability. We need to think like we're a species living with other species.

If this is correct, justice means more than we have acknowledged. Justice now means giving *the whole planet* its due, prizing a viable ecosphere and sharing what's necessary for its health. Just love is still neighbor love, but "neighbor" embraces the human and other-than-human together, today and across future generations for thousands of years. Justice-love embraces "all that participates in being," as the theologian H. Richard Niebuhr said.

"We're all in this together" points up these expanded dimensions. "All" is too little, however. It omits the primal elements of earth, air, fire, and water. Neither does it gather in fungi, flora, fauna, bacteria, microbes, and insects. For most folks, "all" embraces *sapiens* only, creation's apex lounging in leather atop the food chain.

To get solidarity right on a small planet with a big human world, love needs to shed the sovereign stupor of human exceptionalism and recognize *all* the "essential workers" upon which life depends. The vast majority are nonhuman. Apart from the kindness of microbial strangers, we can't live at all—and don't. We're no exception to the law that all species depend on other species. Yet not all in the same way. We're not the protagonist in creation's drama. Life is, with us at the outer edge of sheet 400 of the toilet paper timeline. Step back and you'll see that the largest and most numerous branches on the Tree of Life belong to microbes. Did you know that as many as a billion sit in a spoon of dirt? The better part of life is microbial.

"We're all in this together" needs the microscope for another reason. Big changes affect all *sapiens*, but not in the same way. Just as we don't all breathe the same air (some is polluted; some is not), drink the same water (some is safe; some is not), or eat the same food (some is nutritious; some is not), so also we're in this together in very different ways. We may be in the same storm, but we're not in the same boat.

Human beings are a particular kind of social creature, the kind who is *eco*-social and *geo*-social, at home not only *on* Earth but *with* Earth *in* Earth *as* Earth. We are even *cosmo*-social since Earth—the "geo" part—wouldn't exist without its parental sun and its grandparental galaxy. You are children of the cosmos, at home here and nowhere else.

We experience this immersion from birth. We drink planetary water we did not create from wells we did not dig. We breathe oxygen we did not invent as the gift of plants we didn't invent, either. Our food is from soils we did not form. We communicate in languages passed on to us by others just as we raise the roof in songs others composed, with instruments bequeathed by musicians long gone. We are warmed by clothes we didn't weave and fires we didn't build, with fuel we didn't fabricate.

That we are irreducibly *eco-geo-cosmic-social selves* matters because our collective human presence is now so firm, wide, and fateful that we are coevolutionary with the rest of life on this luminous pebble. Unless Anthropocene citizens come to terms with *eco-geo-cosmo* married to *social* until death us do part, and unless Anthropocene citizens find a way to match their best interests to the interests of the broader community of life, we'll unravel existence and undo ourselves. If flourishing isn't mutual, we'll be here awhile and then gone, taking much with us on an exit ramp to nowhere.

In short, only an expansive sense of self is viable. You and I need to feel, with every breath we take and every star we see, both the intimacy and the immensity of the universe. That includes a sense for the dignity, radiance, and sacredness of it all, including those microbial critters that keep us alive.

I'm closing with a story I love. Titled "Mother Culture," it's about the family life of sperm whales, the world's largest creature with teeth and the one who sports about in the Bible as Leviathan and looms in our psyches as the presence who drove Captain Ahab mad in *Moby-Dick; or, the Whale*.

Ecologist Carl Safina writes a story about Shane Gero, a student of sperm whales who was pleased to tutor Safina on how these massive creatures find meaning and purpose in life. What grabbed me is the meaning Shane himself found with his whales, which all have names and personalities. He tells Safina, "The main thing I've learned from whales is that your experience of the world depends on who you experience the world with. Who you're with makes you who you are. The main lesson the whales have taught me is, your family is the most important thing. Learn from Grandma; love your mom; spend time with your siblings. Spending so much time with the whales has changed how I value the people in my life. Learning what the whales value has helped me learn what I value. Trying to learn what it's like to be a sperm whale I've learned what it's like to be me." Safina responds, "I tell Shane that he sounds like Captain Ahab after twenty years of psychotherapy."

Even without psychotherapy, Shane is wise. The company we keep makes us who we are. In this case, it's because we're mammalian eco-geo-social creatures whose company happens to be sperm whales teaching family values. Self, soul, meaning, and value are all relational, with humans and other-than-humans— even microbial strangers.

Keep the faith. We'll be in touch soon. Slobbery kisses from me and Grandma.

Abrazos!

Grandpa

THE CORE KEEPS SCORE

Dear Spud and Eduardo,

The early letters to Spud (a.k.a. Martín)—where do we hail from, and how did we get here?—left even weightier questions somewhere in Park Slope.

We know what they are: Who are we, anyway? What's the nature of human nature? What does it mean to be human? I promised Martín I'd give these a try. And this time I'm writing both of you because you're both Anthropocene kids.

Does that matter? It could. And it will if your novel geological epoch brings changes to our humanity. Could upended and unruly planetary nature alter human nature?

It might. Past geological shifts certainly affected human evolution. Big changes in the environment and thus in human diet, habitat, and ways of surviving drove changes in human bodies, behaviors, and brains. If Earth changed dramatically, humans changed too.

Of course any major changes, like those in brain cavities, take time. Likely millennia. So your lifetimes won't notice much different about human nature than we Holoceners do unless there's an Anthropocene change directly. That would be a human genome change, together with altered genomes for flora, fauna, and microbes.

Incidentally, altered genomes are the ultimate testimony to the innovative human powers that define the Anthropocene. We can redraft the universal life code itself. DNA scissors could thereby alter human and other nature, big time, and turn nature back on itself to inflect millions of years of evolution. An evolutionary reset.

That dumps bulky questions in our laps. Should we be doing this? Can we trust ourselves with these extraordinary powers? Isn't hacking the genome the ultimate instance of *hubris* since anything that goes wrong is likely wrong forever? Shouldn't we impose limits on our creativity? After all, "can do" doesn't mean "should do." Freedom is not license.

Maybe the old mythic accounts were spot on. Maybe it's possible to know too much—that's the question of the Fall. And maybe we can try too hard, which is the lesson of the Tower of Babel.

But let me return to the Holocene and Anthropocene on human nature.

Let's surmise that the Anthropocene may make not one whit of difference; love as belonging and caring, protecting, nurturing, and sacrificing would be the same, as would loving and being loved as life's ultimate reciprocity.

I also imagine that life as meaning-making, mythmaking, and music-making would carry on just as they have since dark arms and a song lifted the first baby to the waiting gods of a full moon. Likewise, casting about for a bigger story to belong to, a greater cause to serve, and saying "yes to life, in spite of every-thing" would be your story in the Anthropocene as much as it's been ours in the Holocene. So, too, the simple joys, pleasures, and mood swings of routine days, with nothing grand or gran-diose about them. These could fill your days as they have ours.

In short, life goes on. Nothing out of the ordinary arises just because geologists tell us Earth has altered again, even in a big way.

There are, however, themes we've not broached. We can start with whether there is a true, or authentic, human self that crosses cultures and time. If there is, does it slide from Holo-cene to Anthropocene with nary a notice? Maybe, maybe not.

Maybe it doesn't matter. Because, even if you could dial back to the late Holocene, a stark reality would still stare you down—the expanding human imprint on a shrinking planet, with little margin for error. When ours was a big planet with a small *sapien* presence, no sirens screamed as people mishandled land and life in their locale. Resilient nature recovered, and people lived, loved, and died much as before. But when multi-tudes bear down on a shrinking planet together, warning bells sound everywhere. Witness two more degrees Celsius bringing climate cataclysm. The report "Refugees from the Earth" cites an estimate that eventually one-third of the world's popula-tion may have to live outside the areas where civilizations have traditionally been built. They will be planetary refugees, with mass migration trailing a hostile climate. All with but a bump in warming.

In short, life changed through unprecedented human power presses like a branding iron into your years, whether they are Holocene or Anthropocene.

Grandma Nyla's and my generation set all this in motion. We did it with the global integration of growing economic systems and communications, the novelty of weapons of mass destruction, the quadrupling of human numbers in a single century, and abysmal treatment of the planetary environment. We were busy. But not kind.

Still, your times differ from ours as proud Holoceners. And if your times differ, is the human condition changed?

I don't think so. But let's find out: The whole marathon of human history should tell us who we have been, at least to this point. To get at that, here's the favorite assignment I used in ethics classes. I asked students to write their own obituaries.

Try it! How do you want to be remembered? What would you say about yourself that would be recognized by those who appreciated the quirks that made you you? "That was Ed," they might whisper with a smile as they heard stories at your memorial service. "Martín was always happy-go-lucky," they might say of him. Each of you has a core that's apparent to others.

I made that assignment during the 1970s through the 1990s, when entrepreneurial and therapeutic individualism was a prevailing cultural mood. I assumed that self-effected self-fulfillment would shadow the obit assignment, that students' individual attributes and accomplishments would be the focus.

I was startled! Rarely did individualism capture the obituaries. Nor were "résumé" virtues and values front and center. Instead, "eulogy virtues" and "legacy values" were the bright threads. "I was a good husband or wife, father or mother, friend and neighbor. I showered love and care when and where I could.

I gave of my time and talent. I tutored kids. I gave back to family and community." Such was the drift.

Never once did an obituary say, "I climbed to the top of the ladder, pushed past everyone in my high school and college class on the way, made more money than the whole sad lot of them, and spent it as I damn well wished." Considering that self-centered people are legion, and that all of us are self-centered at times, it's startling that what counted in the end, even for egotists-in-training, were legacy values.

The nature of the assignment mattered, I'm sure. While we don't know how our life will unfold in front of us, its final chapter is certain. You can count on death even more than another birthday. That was the point: Write your obituary starting from just before your last breath and watch your life scroll out until it arrives at its sure end. When there are no more second chances, and the only words you have are other people's memories about you, what story do you want told?

Here's my take on the story that we, as a human race, would want as our legacy. See if you think it holds for human nature as we've known it from its earliest scratchings.

An authentic self is unmistakably social. I am a person as a person with others. Any fulfillment I know comes in being with and for them. I want to be remembered for the good I lived in family and community.

Here's backhanded confirmation. When the self is forsaken and alone, it shrinks to a nubbin. We can betray our essential nature as social creatures and do, all the time. Yet, because "social" is core, and the core keeps score, we know in the marrow of our bones that the self that does not love dies.

A letter Albert Einstein wrote late in life confirms the authentic self.

He wrote thousands of letters. This one came decades after his revolutionary insights in physics had earned the respect of his fellow luminaries. He told his old friend Max Born, "I am generally regarded as sort of a petrified object. I find this role not too distasteful, as it corresponds very well with my temperament.... I simply enjoy giving more than receiving in every respect, do not take myself nor the doings of the masses seriously, am not ashamed of my weaknesses and vices, and naturally take things as they come with equanimity and humor."

To "enjoy giving more than receiving in every respect," as well as accepting himself warts and all, and not taking himself too seriously: this was Einstein's authentic self. He enjoyed settling into it. True to himself, he took things as they came "with equanimity and humor." We're this kind of being. "Giving and receiving in every respect" is the still point around which our worlds turn. Normative relationships are mutual, reciprocal, communal. Failing them, we curdle.

You may know that Toni Morrison numbers among my best-ever writers. I'm reminded of something she used to tell her students: "When you get these jobs that you have been so brilliantly trained for, just remember that your real job is that if you are free, you need to free somebody else. If you have some power, then your job is to empower somebody else. This is not just a grab-bag candy game." That's true of you and of me as well. Your life work is freeing and empowering others. Name it your "vocation" or "calling." It, rather than a career, is your true undertaking. Of course, your career might be the vehicle, as writing was for Morrison.

For Ruth Bader Ginsburg, the cause was rooted in the law. Barely five feet tall, she was a titan of the law both when arguing cases before the Supreme Court and as one of its distinguished members. Her career focus was gender equality and equal citizenship for both women and men. But when asked what "a meaningful life" meant, she replied, "To put it simply, it means doing something outside yourself. I tell the law students I address now and then, 'If you're going to be a lawyer and just practice your profession, well you have a skill, so you're very much like a plumber, but if you want to be a true professional, you will do something outside yourself, something to repair tears in your community, something to make life a little better for people less fortunate than you.' That's what I think a meaningful life is, one lives not just for oneself, but for one's community."

These are all legacy values. We see these values in Einstein's emphasizing "giving more than receiving in every respect" rather than his achievements as a celebrity scientist, Morrison telling her students that freeing and empowering others was their real job, and Ginsburg's determination to "repair tears" in the community. In all these, legacy values trump résumé values. It's the African proverb "I am because we are; we are because I am."

I had an epiphany about a shared self in an unlikely place, the Hennepin County Juvenile Detention Center. I worked there for three years, usually 4:00 p.m. to midnight, with each shift split between intake and program. Those years stamped "community" as a theme in your grandpa's writing, teaching, and neighborhood activity. The fragility of community bonds, and the terrible deficits that result when kids lack a healthy community of belonging, never left me. Some of the kids I came to know became loners who had taken up destructive habits. Others sought recognition and "mattering" by joining gangs. The gang became their community and world, rather than family or school, the YMCA, YWCA, or Scouts.

Whatever the path taken, the need for community—and the consequences of having none or having the wrong one—left marks.

My shift partner was Charlie Brown. Yes, the "real" Charlie Brown of *Peanuts* fame. And Charlie looked the part. He was short, with a round head a little large for his body, a locket of hair permanently arced across the forehead, sad brown eyes, and a countenance worthy of those who bear the woes of the world. While Charlie was a serious sort, he was also unfailingly compassionate and always seemed in good, if subdued, spirits. His smile was small but always easy.

Charlie had quit his job as an instructor to designers and artists at the Minneapolis Institute of Art to work with troubled youth. His colleague Charles Schultz quit at the same time to give cartoons a try. Schultz called his first cartoons *Charlie Brown*. The publisher later changed that to *Peanuts: Good Ol' Charlie Brown.*

I'm telling you this because Charlie pulled off a miracle I've only seen once. We all knew the quiet magic that youth felt in his presence. For that matter, anyone in Charlie's presence, youth or staff, felt they were the only ones who mattered during time with him. I've met very few people who were so wholly and quietly present and so willing to accept you as you are.

It wasn't long before I experienced Charlie's calm charisma. Sometimes the detention center's buzzer would sound and at the door would be not a police officer and manacled youth but a former resident or two, now free and "on the outs." They had come by to see their friend Charlie Brown, to catch him up on their lives and let him know how they were doing. They were sure he wanted to know.

I worked a while longer before I learned that Charlie told the judges that youth who had nowhere to go on probation could be released to him. He was single with a large home in Minnetonka. He would accept responsibility for the kids who lived with him until their probationary period was up. The miracle: not one of the youth released to Charlie was ever in trouble again.

Charlie died of cancer at fifty-seven, leaving behind I don't know how many young and not-so-young mourners who had, in his presence, known the kind of care and community that transformed them. They had been shown what they could be. The previous version of who they were was no longer acceptable. That self was misguided, scared, and too small. The person Charlie helped them become was not.

Charlie's a good person with whom to finish this letter and move to the next. Not because he was a saint (though he was) but because he quietly and competently embodied what we all recognize as our core humanity. Rest in peace, Charlie Brown.

Goodnight, you two. Grandma Nyla would love to read you a story and hear your favorite song, as would I. We're counting the days until King Corona lets us come.

Los amo,

Grandpa

WE/THEY R US

Dear Martín and Eduardo,

I have the evening free, so let's carry on. We're trying to tease out the human nature that plots the *sapien* record across time, place, and culture. We're looking for a self that everyone shares.

Tonight's thesis is that the authentic self is not only eco-geo-social; it's tribal.

I suppose I unknowingly mentioned the tribal self when we talked about Charlie Brown and the detention center youth who were gang members. Tough as their bravado made them sound, they yearned to be part of something beyond the emptiness they knew too well. The gang answered.

We are all gang members by nature. We don't call our people gangs or cliques, but they are. We might say "my community," "my friends," "my country," or "my people," but each mimics a gang and a clique in that each is a community to which we belong body and soul.

We could also say "my tribe." Tribalism is a human constant. It's "we" vis-à-vis "they" in a thousand guises that distinguish "us" from "them." Memberships can change, and often do, but universal inclusivity never replaces tribalism. We don't belong equally to all.

Tribalism has a lot going for it. One reason is that we can't live without simplifying.

A quip making the rounds among ecologists has it about right: As for complexity, human society is to the rainforest what the squeak of a mouse is to the history of music. Or, to cite a soil scientist, "Eco-systems are not only more complex than we think; they are more complex than we can *ever* think." So we trim, cut, paste, reduce, and adapt biodiverse, infinitely complex nature for human ends. We domesticate and mass produce a few select animals and crops because simplification is far more efficient and manageable for us. That it's far less efficient and manageable for the rest of the natural world doesn't enter the equation.

Simplifying is what we do. It's who we are.

We simplify human populations as well but in a certain way. We lump them according to some trait or other we then ascribe to the group as a whole, whether or not it holds for individuals or even for the majority of the lumped. Lumps may be sorted by race, class, gender, age, nationality, culture, history, language, or some mix. Friend or enemy, ally or opponent, native or foreigner, exotic or pedestrian, beautiful or ugly, add further divisions.

This is "othering," and it typically falls on differences rather than sameness. Everyone does it. We all simplify; we all lump. This flattens the complex differences that exist in every group of human beings in favor of a few shared ones we use to create stereotypes. Stereotypes then prejudge members of any "they" group we come across (women are . . . ; Hispanics speak . . . ; rich people prefer . . . ; Somalis like . . . ; Germans always . . . ; etc.). This prejudging is, as the word indicates, "prejudicial." And it's panhuman; everyone prejudges.

Prejudging resists complexity, shirks nuance, and turns harmful when the prejudicial group has power. Prejudice plus power creates privilege, which then digs in to set the norms and have its way.

Here's a little more. Simplifying reflects creaturely limits. We *sapiens* cannot take in all that is. Our minds cannot process the full complexity of, say, the rainforest or, for that matter, most any vibrant human culture not our own. We can see as far as the horizon but not over it. Even close up, some things are too small for bare eyes and too numerous to count, even in our own body (like atoms, genes, and cells). Far off, some things are too big to accommodate sight and mind and too deviant to fit the categories we use (like planets that are gases, not rocks, and the mysterious dark matter saturating most of space). Even with super-technologies that transcend human limitations, we feed the data into models we have or might create. The simplifying algorithms and equations are ours, as are the systems that channel the outcome.

In short, simplifying, sorting, lumping, and othering look like durable human features. You should count on that for the Anthropocene while remembering that we/they memberships can change, dramatically. And those changes can matter, dramatically.

There's nothing wrong with group membership as such. We belong nowhere until we belong somewhere, and somewhere is never everywhere. Tribalism per se isn't inherently bad, though it has dynamics that easily yield to our own tribe having preeminent value but not "the other." "We" are ranged over against "them" with the proviso that norm-making is in the hands of the collective "we." We find meaning in belonging to our tribe while bolstering that meaning by denigrating other tribes.

I cannot know what your tribal memberships will be and the company you keep that will make you you. I do know that tribalism often results in double standards. The very same patterns have played out across all the big issues just in the last year—racial reckoning, the effects of the pandemic, class and inequality, women's work and status, the rollout of vaccinations, climate change legislation, and more. These similar patterns of injustice are far less the consequences of individual traits and intentions and far more the result of structures and systems of group life. By way of guiding narratives and institutions, systems and laws, good people work evil in highly efficient, routine ways. (In my day we called the double standards, the patterns of injustice, and the elevation of our tribe and our own species to the denigration of others "sin." What do you call it?)

The two of you will have lived the downstream consequences of humans viewing themselves as set-apart masters of their own fate and the fate of other life. Rabbi Abraham Joshua Heschel has it right: "Cloistered in our own concepts, we may scorn and revile everything." My tribe cloistered itself in our own concepts and bordered itself off from the totality of being. We suffocated ourselves and other life in our little species-isolated world. That, too, is sin.

Has that lesson come too late? Maybe. Sometimes it feels like all I do all day long is hope that species pride and arrogance have not wholly ravaged your world.

OK, where are we? What human nature persists across time, place, and culture?

Perhaps this. We are born with love coming more naturally from the human heart than hate, as Nelson Mandela said, and we are by nature good, big-hearted, and other-oriented. We are also eco-geo-social selves, creatures of a wondrous cosmic web. But we are limited as well, always parochial and tribal despite powers of imagination and intellect that seem boundless. Are we also constitutionally flawed? It seems so in that there is no human platform without a shadow side. Yet none has ever existed that did not practice love, either. Each of us individually and all of us together seem a paradox, even to ourselves.

So is paradoxically the only way to be human? Apparently. I suspect that won't be different for you in the Anthropocene.

I'm breaking off now. The birds need to be fed, the mail fetched, and a salad assembled for dinner. I'll be back tomorrow.

Los amo,

Grandpa

ALL TOO HUMAN

July 16, 2020

Dear Eduardo and Spud,

Are you in day camp in the park? The one that acts out Greek myths? I'm happily stuck in a writing mood, so I'll pick up from yesterday's letter.

A British newspaper invited readers to answer the question "What's wrong with the world today?" Here's one reply.

Dear sir,

I am.

Yours,

G. K. Chesterton

Chesterton was certain that a flawed humanity admitted no exceptions. Blemished is the kind of creature we are, no matter who, when, or where. So we respond to some bumbling with "it's all too human." All too common, predictable, normal, unfortunate. (I think it was Mark Twain who said that the worst advice you can give anyone is "Just be yourself.")

Still, "all too human" reveals more than we give it credit. It's more than what we just described. "Too human" is the reason that tales as age-old as Cain and Abel, Joseph and his brothers, Odysseus, Oedipus Rex, and Antigone circle back around. "All too human" camps out in every Shakespeare play, in children's stories, in Harry Potter's adventures, and those of Frodo Baggins in The Lord of the Rings series. Judging from their following, in Marvel Comics too.

Both of you have books about your favorite superheroes. Do they seem real? And, Eduardo, you've been reading Greek and Nordic myths. Do those characters seem human?

Ages come and go, but human nature budges little and its flaws not at all. As Buddhists are wont to say, "Before Enlightenment, the laundry; and after Enlightenment, the laundry." But which flaws carry the day, with what outcomes, matters mightily. They can parse life from death.

The same goes for strokes of genius and acts of solidarity. Genius, goodness, solidarity, chutzpah, creativity, and resilience are all human too. I know we don't associate these positives with "all too human." But we should, not least because these positives may take on salient Anthropocene dimensions you will know but Grandma Nyla and I did not.

That pivots the discussion from constancies in human nature to variations in human culture. By "culture," I mean the stuff we do that adds up to the way we live. Culture is the beliefs, practices, technologies, philosophy, social norms, and wisdom that create a people's way of life.

Cultural diversity and possibility could mean everything to you. If biodiversity allows adaptations to change in the natural world, cultural diversity seems its counterpart for the eco- and geo-human world. It's your talent pool for meeting Darwin's challenge—"It is not the strongest of the species that survives, nor the most intelligent that survives, but the one that is most adaptable to change." Cultural diversity lets you keep changing.

Not that dogged human nature will fade. Culture doesn't repeal or replace human nature. Quite the contrary, cultural variety expresses it.

How so? Take a look.

Humans are always breaking the molds. Custom and social cohesion have their day, but they don't last. Impermanence reigns because we are an incurably restless species that lives across a gap arcing from "is" to "could be" to "ought." Sometimes dramatically, sometimes subtly, sometimes barely at all, we keep prying open possibilities we've not yet entertained or that have been sidelined or lost. So when the present course seems bound for a dead end, we try to crack history open again. Or at least make a dent.

We also try to undo injustice and injury that should not have occurred in the first place. Racism, for example, "should never have happened and so you don't get a cookie for reducing it." Racial injustice is unacceptable history. Repair alone is acceptable, even in the face of entrenched resistance from those who narrate their blemished story as one of their superior valor.

Boys, take note here. A narrative of valor is often a trap its creators set for themselves. The writer James Baldwin declared, "People who imagine that history flatters them (as it does, since they wrote it) are impaled on their history like a butterfly on a pin and incapable of seeing or changing themselves, or the world."

But whether we face a past that should never have been or a future that has not yet broken from its cocoon, the soul's agitation continues. Some days we're discontented, angry, and sullen. Other days we're inspired, adventuresome, and full of good ideas. Yet we never tarry indefinitely. We rally to tweak the mold, break it, or set it aside as a has-been.

Persistent as human restlessness is, it comes with a deceptive yearning for security and stability. It feeds a conviction that what we've created is here to stay and shouldn't be messed with. How many rebels believed their revolution was the last one necessary and their utopia written in the stars?

In 1992, Francis Fukuyama published *The End of History and the Last Man.* While it already looks quaint to me, it will seem plain silly to you. *The End of History* was a runaway bestseller that followed in the wake of the dramatic fall of state-sponsored socialism across Eastern Europe and the Soviet Union. Fukuyama claimed that the triumph of liberal democratic capitalist societies cut in a Western mode rendered them irreversible and permanent. US president Ronald Reagan and British prime minister Margaret Thatcher claimed the same with a popular acronym, TINA—There Is No Alternative!

But in doing so they fundamentally misjudged human nature. Because we *sapiens* are both finite and free, limited and imaginative, unhappy with our lot and transcendent of it, we disrespect every endpoint to history. Germany's Thousand-Year Reich lasted twelve years. The Roman Empire did much better, but it, too, is long gone. Empires large and small share the same fate: they all fall. Rather than "No Alternative," the motto should be "There Is Always an Alternative." TIAA.

In fairness to Fukuyama, he knew things could go awry, and might. But he wrongly thought that the framework of Western democracy and economy was firmly in place. He underestimated the innate, restless freedom that is expressed in the seemingly endless variety of human cultures and subcultures. *The End of History* is fantasy.

You two and your compatriots can count on this creative restlessness.

Cultural creativity and diversity seem the makings of a fruitful survival strategy. Especially if, instead of empire or other forms of giantism, you design life from your own localities and their varied assets, for the sake of sustainable community in the places you live. Rather than "there is no alternative," there are thousands.

This will not end in the Anthropocene. On the contrary, Anthropocene crises may send unbound creativity soaring since brute necessity is the busy mother of invention.

Here's the complication that keeps me awake. When Earth itself has set off on a different course, the same actions from which Nyla and I and millions of others benefited may generate very different outcomes for you. The grim side of that was voiced in the first letter to Eduardo where I said that Anthropocene citizens who continue Holocene habits doom their own children. We seem bent on trapping ourselves in our own do-it-yourself cage and impaling ourselves on our own history like a butterfly on a pin, as Baldwin cautioned.

The greatest peril of climate system change is "that the accidental powers of humanity generate problems that exceed our moral imagination and defeat our abilities to take responsibility." Human nature may remain the same, yet collective human activity puts us where we cannot truly take responsibility for the powers we wield. We unleash chaos we can no longer control. In the name of a better civilization, we undermine the one we have.

I don't know if this will come to pass, and I won't be around to find out. But it troubles me no end because if it happens, you, whom we love with no modesty whatsoever, will live it. In any event, I seem to get nowhere that doesn't loop back to how dogged human nature is. Still, I want to hold out for a transformation in the human condition. How else will you rise to Anthropocene challenges?

Los amo,

Grandpa

DIFFERENT ALL THE SAME

August 7, 2020

Dear Eduardo, dear Martín,

Eduardo, your folks sent a video. You're reading one of your books aloud. We didn't see the title, but an elephant seems to be the main character.

Your diction is polished in English and Spanish, so it took us a couple of minutes to figure out why we didn't understand you. You were reading words backward a phrase at a time. Maybe this is the secret language of the mythical kingdom of Eduardolandia. I know Eduardolandia has its own tongue. Is it English or Spanish backward? We'll check with you.

Your creativity with language poses a good question. How did this come to be? Not just for you but as a human possibility at all? At least to date, we know of no other species who reads or writes children's books. Or grown-ups' books, for that matter. It's possible, I guess, that some future nonhuman species might do that or that aliens on an exoplanet already do. So far as we know, however, only humans do here. (Even fewer pronounce the words backward and read them in reverse order. You're in a class by yourself.)

What's going on, then, with you and your backward English or Spanish? Help us out here. Why should scratches on paper, papyrus, or animal hide mean something? Why should sounds we make as we exhale in the open air form words that channel thoughts originating somewhere in the mush of our brains?

It's because this is language, and we're language creatures. Other creatures communicate, too, and have what we might call "languages" of their own. Right now, there's a raucous conversation outside my office window. It's distinct noises from birds perched on the feeder and those who would like to take their place. The sounds are different, depending on the species, but all seem to understand what the cacophony is about. Still, none of the birds reads feeder rules from a manual they wrote. And they don't have numbers flashed on the adobe wall to show who goes next. Nor have rabbits down the hillside posted "Keep Out! No Trespassing!" signs for coyotes, at least those coyotes who read English.

Unlike birds, we humans are creatures of language that takes the form of thousands of seemingly arbitrary ensembles of sounds in the air called "talking" and scratches on the page called "writing." Written language, though not spoken language, is unique to *Homo sapiens*.

Yet language is only one expression of what makes us who we are as modern humans. And this in spite of the DNA we share with the rest of life and the same cellular processes that point to a common ancestor for all planetary life. We're the same in so many elemental respects. Yet we're all different, too, even unique.

To be is to be different. That is evolution's story, for us and all else. "Different's the commonest thing going." We're not on the same evolutionary ladder. We're on different tracks, like different branches and twigs in a different part of the tree. But how are we different? Human singularity is *a certain kind of consciousness.* It's the kind of consciousness that plays with language, makes up fanciful stories, and creates mythical kingdoms at a young (or old) age. It's five-year-olds reading words backward and the story in reverse, to their own delight and with a few giggles aimed at parents. And, Eduardo, if you notice your dad's interest flagging, remind him that when he was your age, he spent hour upon hour making up stories, many with secret friends.

Here's a "dad story" that shows how language brings into the open the unique human consciousness that surfaces early on.

In our Washington, DC, row house, the bedrooms were on the second floor. Your dad's was down the hallway from ours, with bunk beds so that he could have a friend over. Bedtime routine found him crawling into bed with the light on so we could read a story, sing a song together, and say a goodnight prayer. We might also talk for a while about the day just ending or what was in store for the morrow. But at some point he'd say, "OK, Dad, you can turn on the dark now." Not "turn off the light" but "turn on the dark."

Darkness was as real as light and evidently good as well. It wasn't scary, and no effort was made to banish it. It belonged to the day's rhythm and would live up to its responsibility for a good night's sleep. "OK, Dad, you can turn on the dark now" was as logical as "You can turn off the light." This was consciousness with matchless room for twists and turns that children play with as they learn the world.

Not that consciousness itself is humanly unique. Most creatures are conscious and respond to their environment in nuanced and sophisticated ways, some more nuanced and sophisticated than ours. Many see better, smell better, run faster, jump higher, taste with more discrimination, and, in the case of birds, fly a whole lot better. That beloved companion, the horse, is bigger, faster, and stronger than any human. But no creature you can name is mindful and imaginative in the way of five-year-olds.

To be sure, we are all part of the same progression of life forms. Remember how so many species, in the oceans and on land, evolved from fish?

Yet something sets us apart. Take Spud, a.k.a. Martín, this past week in the park. He finds a stick. It could be a broken, bare tree branch and no more. But within minutes it's a tool for digging. He doesn't have any seeds along, so it isn't the digging stick human communities used for centuries to plant crops. But digging is fun with or without seeds.

For a while. Then the stick becomes a wand. Exactly what magic it performs isn't clear from Spud's squeals. But he seems to know that waving the wand around in every direction while turning in circles creates an imaginary world into something that borders on the real.

Yet "wand" isn't the last chapter. The stick is a weapon too. Right now it's for scaring robins just when they're finding worms after last night's rain. Fortunately the stick is not for hitting other kids, at least not yet, or for thrusting at Dad's leg. Instead it's a walking stick, like Grandpa's, and that lasts for the half-hour walk home.

Martín is not willing to leave his stick outside, however, and it becomes a cane to pound each stair to the fourth floor. Then—voilà!—with your help, Eduardo, a part of it is broken into small pieces to become freight for his beloved train.

Tool, wand, weapon, walking stick, cane, building material, and freight—who knew that a two-year-old had all that figured out before he could explain it to anybody else? Except maybe "Mine! Mine! It's mine!"

Spud stands in for all the "bipeds with the giant dreams" in the evolutionary account. One of them looked at a broken branch and a stone and saw a hammer and a hunting tool. Another looked at shells and saw money—a certain number of the right shells could be traded for a bow and arrow. Still another looked at a tree and imagined her whole family branching like that, a family tree.

These are all symbols, one thing standing for another. *Sym* means "together"; *bole* means a "throw." Sym-bols throw together some object or action and some image or word for it in order to create a meaning that the symbol then conveys as shorthand. Maybe the symbol is utilitarian and no more—Martín's digging stick, a red octagon for a stop sign, a white H on a blue shield for a hospital. But a symbol might also be evocative—a wedding ring, a family heirloom, a war memorial, a treasured photograph, a flag. Some are horrific—a swastika or a noose.

Language is one of the most elaborate and highly complex of these symbol systems. A musical score is another. Otherwise meaningless sounds and scratches suddenly give voice to complex worlds.

While these examples and thousands more are distinct in appearance, sound, and meaning, the dynamic is ever the same. Things are "thrown together"—images and representations, gestures, words, objects, and actions—in order to create, convey, mark, evoke, sustain, or change meaning.

That's symbolic consciousness, and it's the way we map the world. It's how we communicate what we see, do, and imagine.

It's *how* we are *who* we are. It's the human thing, and it's magnificent. It's the way you two will remap and remake the world.

The consciousness of big-dreaming bipeds is also self-aware. Spud with his stick is probably in his chimp stage. Chimpanzees, too, look at a stick and see a tool or a weapon. And if you edited videos of chimps at play and Martín at play, you could splice them so that each takes the other's place. The play would be much the same. Likewise, Martín's face-plant on his mother's breast for a quick snack has its counterpart in chimp culture.

Too, Martín over this last year has become his own person. He's become an individual. Jane Goodall, who camped out with chimps for decades, says chimps become individuals too. Some make their own bed at night. They display intelligence. They have personalities. So do elephants, octopi, and even pigs. While their intelligence isn't a free-range match of ours, they are intelligences of their own.

Yet chimps and these other animals don't grow into what Spud will. An explosion of mind makes the difference—mind as intellect and mind as imagination, together. Martín will become a self-aware person capable of reflecting on the whole expanse of his life and much, much more. He'll contemplate the distant past, an imaginary future, other lives and other worlds, the void at the end of life, and the gap that gives rise to morality itself, the gap between what is and what could and ought to be. He will, in short, acquire the kind of consciousness that can explore a vast reality and be keenly aware of himself in the process.

Self-aware, reflective symbolic consciousness is the means. Science and religion, art and myth, language and story are the creations. They belong to the kind of creatures we are. So far as we know to date, neither chimps nor any other

DIFFERENT ALL THE SAME

creatures possess such complex, deliberative, self-reflective, and exploratory minds.

Whether other mammalian relatives are not only self-aware but death-aware is a question. Some may be death-aware in the moving way that, say, elephants are. Elephants mourn, even half-bury, their dead. And they empathize with family members who suffer. They know grief and fear. They cooperate to extend help, too, pushing a youngster to safety from the mudhole where the little one is stuck in the muck.

Without doubt they are community creatures with shared emotions. Nyla and I were with South African friends watching a couple dozen elephants at a watering hole. Suddenly behind us we heard what sounded like shrieks of joy and then pounding, earth-shaking feet as a second group came running to the waterhole. They weren't headed for the water, however. They came for a reunion, fondling the little ones, nudging against the adults, throwing their trunks into the air and flapping their big ears, all a din of elephant music. They acted like long-lost family and friends now partying. Intimacy, recognition, joy and emotion reigned.

Yet even if their gathering had been a sad one—an elephant death and quasi-funeral—I'm quite certain that human death-awareness holds a further dimension.

Recall the obituary assignment. Descartes's "I think, therefore I am" says that I can doubt everything but not myself. I cannot doubt the consciousness that doubts all else. Yet "I think, therefore I am" is shadowed by "I am, therefore I die." That I will cease to be is the driving impetus for leaving behind something meaningful (like these letters to you!). We want something of who we are to outlive our numbered days—a family who will remember us with affection and stories, a collection of photographs and family heirlooms, a last will and testament, maybe a planted tree and a planned memorial service. We resist disappearing without a trace.

This is more than fighting for our lives. Every creature does that. This is marking and remembering our days and letting others know they should remember them too.

Still, I'm not out to dig a ditch between us and our mammalian relatives. We share the same force that animates all life. We all need earth, air, fire, and water. We share similar ways of having offspring and caring for them. Many also have minds, personalities, and emotions we recognize as parallel to ours. Not least, we are creatures of purpose led by intent who are descended from other creatures of purpose led by intent. We're part of the same crowd.

I am arguing instead that being death-aware as part of being self-aware goes very deep for *sapiens*. Being stands out from nonbeing like something contrasts with nothing and meaning fights emptiness. I am no psychologist, but I suspect that, more than other critters, humans know deep down that nothingness might be our fate when we've breathed our last, if not before. We resist that void with all that we have, and we act accordingly, even if it's only to say a cheery "good morning" at the start of the day and turn on the radio to confirm that the world is still out there.

Maybe I'm making too much of self-awareness as also death-awareness and of death-awareness, conscious and unconscious, as what keeps us going and happy to still be here. But there's a point. It's that self-awareness joins symbolic and reflective consciousness as *how* we are *who* we are. Surely that won't be different for you.

Let's leave it at that and move to something different. We've stared at ourselves long enough and probably overstayed our welcome. It's time to turn our gaze elsewhere. In the next letter.

Meanwhile, I'm off to brush my teeth and crawl into bed with a good book. After that, I'll turn on the dark.

Be well, dear children. Eduardo, don't forget to tell us the title of the elephant book you read backward. Grandma Nyla sends her love and hugs to both of you too.

Los amo,

Grandpa

WHAT'S IN A NAME IF THE NAME IS GOD?

September 5, 2020

Dear Martín,

What's in a name? Yours and your brother's are long: Eduardo Maximiliano Rasmussen-Villegas and Martín Theo Rasmussen-Villegas.

I can't do much with Eduardo's name, although we know Maximilian was the immigrant in Grandma Nyla's family who came to the States. Family lore is that he was a stowaway on a ship to New York. Probably illegal, that one.

Your middle name is another matter—Theo from *theos*, Greek for "God." So let's you and I commit a little theology together.

Theology is simply God-talk. More precisely, and because it's an "–ology," theology is the *study* of God-talk. It's talk *about* God, not *to* God.

I do talk about God from time to time. Recall my appreciative mention of Rabbi Nahum's translation of God as "Living Presence." Because Living Presence is a hovering love covering all that is, it's all but impossible not to be in the midst of it.

"Everyone who loves is born of God and knows God" is John's version. Since few would never experience love, few would never experience Living Presence. We can't be where God isn't.

But I'm also aware of Hebrew reticence about uttering the name of the Ineffable or thinking God can be captured by name. Moses tries. He asks God's name. The response? "I Am Who I Am." The mysterious name isn't an answer at all, just fog. (Is the fogginess deliberate?)

I treasure the humility and awe that arrest the human attempt to capture the God Moses cannot name and dare not see face to face. My reluctance arises elsewhere, however, with the fifth-century saint and bishop, Augustine.

Time with Augustine started with his political thought in a grad school course, and I've come back to him often since, not least because he has credentials as an early eco-theologian. Augustine calls the common elements that make for life "standing miracles"—earth and sky, water, our bodies, and nature comprehensively. These "standing miracles" are "a greater miracle than the rarest and most unheard-of marvels." God, like the devil, is in the details. Gloriously so.

Not that Augustine found the Pax Romana attentive to standing miracles. The only joy attained in the Empire had "the fragile brilliance of glass, a joy outweighed by the fear that it may be shattered in a moment."

Potential paradise is nevertheless hidden in miraculous Earth, he says, with "seeds waiting for the light of justice and mercy." When justice and mercy shine, the world is "a smiling place." (A fine emoji for the world of our dreams!)

Earth as just and merciful is the alternative to empire for Augustine. While he is sometimes cozy with empire, he never found the empire "a smiling place" and never shrank from sharp words about it. Why do you "infest the Earth," he asks the oppressive rich. Earth was given by God as common for the use of all, yet under rule by the wealthy, Earth has suffered imperial "infestation."

Yet it's Augustine's caution about God-talk that brings me up short: "If you think you understand, it is not God you're talking about." Here, Augustine joins the conviction that we can never know about God with certainty and perhaps not at all. Who can know the Unknowable? Listen to that again: "If you think you understand, it is not God you're talking about."

But I suggested we commit some theology, and the term for this tradition is *apophatic* theology. Like your middle name, *theos*, *apophasis* is Greek and literally means "saying away." The word acknowledges that God escapes our concepts, so the best we can manage is to say what or who God is *not* on our way to encountering the God *beyond* our knowing. (Hey, that's a start.)

We cannot say what or who God is, however. Even for *Homo sapiens*, the brainy species, our finite mammalian minds and small-world knowledge cannot grasp the Ineffable or know the Unknowable. Finite limits put the Infinite out of reach.

A warning label accompanies religions resting in the bosoms of Abraham, Sarah, and Hagar—the warning that any departures from humility, any bold claims about knowing God, end in idol-making. Human hearts and minds run busy little factories that substitute things limited, partial, and human-centered for things ultimate, whole, and divine. The substitutes are idols.

Creating self-serving idols is not our only desire. More power than should be entrusted to fallibility is another. This will-to-power creates God or gods in our own image and then claims their sanction for what we do and who we are. Consequently, the most dangerous *sapiens* are those certain they know God's will and have God as their ally. Religion then ratchets up certitude to a fever pitch that fuels punishing laws, crusades, and theocracy.

Certitude is a perversion of faith. Faith isn't about living with certainty; it's about being confident, even joyous, about living with intractable uncertainty and profound mystery. Absolute certainty has no need of faith.

Here is a truth I've learned: Whoever, whatever, or however God is, God is not an item on an inventory of the universe. Yet most of us make God an object.

Language hits a bump here. To say, as I just did, that "God is" or "God is not" is already to turn God into an object. "Is" identifies an object, an entity, a thing, and it's one object among others.

That's profoundly wrong. And while I don't expect you, me, or anyone else to give up saying "God is" or "is not" this or that, let's recognize that such talk is mistaken.

Here's why. Religious language is all metaphor, symbol, simile, parable, and story. None of those bears literal objectivity, none trades in hard measurable fact, none tests its claims in the rigorous manner of science. As if intuiting the limits of mind and language, religious faith says that God is *like* . . . like a rock, an eagle, a lamb, a shepherd, a sunrise, a song, a mighty fortress, a woman in search of a lost coin, the father of a prodigal, a mighty wind, a loving embrace, or Father, Son, Holy Spirit. At least with metaphors, similes, analogies, parables, and stories, we don't say God *is*, objectively, any of these entities. We say that only in *some* way God is *akin* to some feature they display at a particular time in particular circumstances that are experienced by particular human beings. For God-talk, *like* is as good as it gets.

So let's acknowledge, then, that "Living Presence," too—a.k.a. "God"—is feeble language attempting to name the Unnamable. Living Presence is a lovely but imperfect way to address Great Mystery. By "mystery," I don't mean what we do not know (though some of that is there) but mystery as what we sense deeply about the whole.

Even apart from God-talk, the limits of language apply. Toni Morrison is splendid on this. What language does is "reach," she says. Language reaches, but it can't pin things down: "Its force, its felicity, is in its reach toward the ineffable." Yet it never quite arrives. So we search for yet other words to grasp the same mystery. They don't quite arrive, either. Great Mystery is never fully pinned down.

Despite reaching but never arriving, naming will continue. Lost in both wonder and finitude, humans have always felt that something envelops us. *Theos* in a thousand guises is the name we give that; a thousand guises is what's in a name when the name is "God."

Martín—"Spud" is actually my favorite name for you—I guess this means I should confess the God I *don't* believe in. It's the same one, I discover, that many atheists and agnostics disavow.

Here's anthropologist Gregory Bateson's statement, from 1972:

If you put God outside and set him vís-a-vís his creation and if you have the idea that you are created in his image, you will logically and naturally see yourself outside and against the things around you. And as you arrogate all mind to yourself, you will see the world around you as mindless and therefore not entitled to moral or ethical consideration. The environment will seem yours to exploit.

While I was not raised on exactly this God, mine was a kissin' cousin. At Union State Line Lutheran Church in Petersburg, God *was* a God apart. We humans were created in His image (and God was always "He"), and we, too, were outside and over all else as object. We also arrogated all mind to ourselves. Nature was subject to our minds and technologies—tractors, plows, threshing machines, milk machines, loans from the bank, and baling wire.

Humans were separate from the rest of nature and set over "it." The good folk of Petersburg did not view "the environment" as ours "to exploit," however. Reverence and a sense of Christian stewardship took the edge off that. God entrusted the environment to us as a gift to care for.

This tempered our stance. Farmers knew we couldn't make a single blade of pasture grass from scratch, much less an oak tree, with its nests and birds. And they knew that in every seed, the biblical bush still burned. Yes, they could plant the seeds and help grow the crops. But water, soil, sunshine, and seeds were out of their hands. I remember their words: "We prepare the ground but God gives the increase."

Even the farmers we kids loved to hear swear around the pool table in Dad's gas station had this sense of the divine. To hear them tell of the birth of a calf that morning, you'd think it was holy. It was. I doubt that the Lutheran church—the only church in Petersburg—ever shared Luther's word that "all creatures are sacraments," but these cantankerous farmers had a feel for that nonetheless.

Mother Nature could be mean, though. Make a helluva mess. They knew that too. Hail might take out crops in an afternoon. The increase God gave could disappear in hours.

For the Petersens, my farmer relatives, the animals were on familial terms. Horses *always* had names and respect just short of baptism. The cows, pigs, and even chickens had names, at least the roosters. Their names were called aloud, and they were treated with affection and care. Grandpa Petersen even kidded his chickens (but he kidded everybody). And he rather enjoyed scolding them for bad behavior, like making a stinky mess in nests he'd given loving attention. "You should know better," he'd say.

All this said, God on the farm was the transcendent God set over "His" creation, with us hard-working folk created in "His" image and exercising dominion responsibly and with gratitude.

That was "mixed farming," family farms of mixed animals and mixed crops, the kind my mom, grandparents, uncles, and aunts cared for in Minnesota and your Grandma Nyla's family cared for in Nebraska. Yet by the time Nyla and I were finishing college, mixed farming was being supplanted with large, corporate-owned mono-crop farms and massive feedlots for single breeds of cattle or hogs. Agri-*business* replaced agri-*culture*.

With that, the relationships changed. No names for the place or for the animals were desired, considered, or needed. No affection either. I never heard anyone doing industrialized agriculture speak of "the homestead" and tell stories of the ancestors who had struggled there. The new purveyors couldn't since they didn't know the ancestors and hadn't homesteaded the land. And God didn't give the increase; Monsanto did. Bateson goes on:

> If this is your estimate of your relation to Nature [humans arrogating all mind to themselves as God's trustees] and *you have an advanced technology*, your likelihood of survival will be that of a snowball in hell. You will die either of the toxic by-products of your own hate, or simply of over-population and overgrazing. . . . If I am right, the whole of our thinking about what we are and what other people are has got to be restructured.

That was 1972. That "the whole of our thinking" has "to be restructured" was said shortly before, on Earth Day in 1970 by organizer Denis Hayes, and has been said many times since. But my point is that the transcendent God who sanctions humankind in this role as God's own image is no longer the one I believe in. I join atheists and agnostics in granting Him gracious leave.

I've abandoned other gods. I'll confess those in future letters. Stay tuned, Martín Theo.

Te amo,

Grandpa

COMING OF AGE

September 10, 2020

Dear Martin Theo,

Earlier I mentioned Dietrich Bonhoeffer, a victim of the Nazis. I never leave home without Dietrich. He attracts me when white privilege is profoundly challenged. The reason's this: he was a culturally and morally conservative patriot who took sober stock of his own beloved culture and, finding it criminal, took life-risking action for a different regime and way of life.

We've talked often about the planetary emergency you face. Bonhoeffer's time was different: climate system change hadn't yet appeared. But his questions about God arose from the same place, namely unprecedented human power affecting all life. While he had no vocabulary for ecology and the Anthropocene, he cut to the heart of both with scalpel precision.

In 1932, a year before Hitler was even in office, Bonhoeffer saw the danger. The German people had been primed for national hubris by their assumption that they embodied an advanced, enlightened, industrial civilization, one that could conquer nature as well as other peoples. Bonhoeffer said that an aggressive "war-and-industry" identity had its sources in the West's battles "to master nature, fight against it, to force it to its service." He diagnosed this assertive mastery as "the fundamental theme of European-American history."

This is more than a battle against nonhuman nature; it's also against other human beings. "In the most essential sense his life means 'killing,'" Bonhoeffer said bluntly of the European. In other words, Euro-American civilization, fragmented from the rest of nature and set over against it in its core consciousness and practices, destroys natural and human communities together in an exercise of collective power with few moral and spiritual constraints. *This is mastery that knows no limits as undertaken by autonomous humans in the name of freedom without constraint.* (This modernity lives on still.)

For Bonhoeffer, such unprecedented human knowledge and power and their actual and potential harm compelled a new ethic of responsibility.

Now jump to 1944, after Bonhoeffer had been imprisoned by the Nazis. "World-come-of-age" is a new phrase in his letters. To "come of age" is to become an adult before the law and take on responsibility for one's life and actions. In our country, this will happen to you when you turn eighteen. From then on, your parents will no longer be responsible for you in the way they are right now. Yet Bonhoeffer never says "person-come-of-age." He says "world-come-of-age." The human world is now wholly responsible for its knowledge and powers, choices, and paths.

Nobody bails us out, including God. Bonhoeffer rejects the rescuer God, the *deus es machina* who in classical drama dropped from the sky to provide a fix when humans needed it but could not provide it. To turn to that God in a time of greatly expanded human powers is a moral cop-out. It sidesteps or deflects human responsibility. Bonhoeffer finds any fill-in-the-blanks God and any last-resort God irresponsible.

Yet these world-come-of-age powers—Anthropocene powers—lack a viable faith and ethic to guide them, so moral imagination and responsibility must be redone. To start with, there can be no dialing back to some previous age. For Christians, constructive work in a new era must question long-standing premises. Who is God, and what do we really believe? How do we exercise power and knowledge so as to find God in what we *do* know, rather than in what we don't (Bonhoeffer's God-of-the-gaps), and in problems that *are* solved, rather than only when and where we are vexed? Moral accountability will address *the sins of our strengths and powers, rather than our weaknesses only.* If God and standing before God in the Anthropocene cannot be located at the heart *of* human power, accountability, accomplishment, and failure, then God and morality are both pushed to the margins of what truly counts for our lives and the life of the world.

God is not an object or a separate being for Bonhoeffer, either. Instead, God is concretely experienced in "being there for others." What's transcendent is not some far-off infinite power but what you experience in life with your neighbor. We don't need religion—a pejorative word for Bonhoeffer. We need the God who enters into suffering in the way of Jesus, bringing life to the wounded and broken places, nature's included.

Bonhoeffer's not the only theologian who saw the kind of theology we would need for the Anthropocene. Joseph Sittler, a Lutheran like Bonhoeffer, was another. In 1970, he was among the very first to recognize the challenge ecology brought to theology, ethics, and society. He wanted people to think

THE PLANET YOU INHERIT

about God and nature very differently than they had before, grounded in a new *relationship* to the world. "I have never been able to entertain a God-idea which was not integrally related to the fact of chipmunks, squirrels, hippopotamuses, galaxies, and light years!" he declared. We and all else are inherently part of everything. Being is, by nature, relational. Reality is "ecological."

This means that creation is not all about us. We are not its reason for being, its apex, or its endpoint. For God, all matter matters.

Boys, I find myself here: I have no attachment to any God who doesn't gather in the entire journey of the universe. God-talk that doesn't encompass all 13.8 billion years of the universe's pilgrimage to date and the immense wheeling of one hundred billion galaxies swimming with stars and planets is stillborn. God-talk that doesn't gather in all species come and gone, as well as those leaving as we speak, and God-talk that doesn't embrace the whole of the drama of life in all its misery, tragedy, and grandeur, is simply quaint. Shorn of the universe, the worship of God is worship of a human idol. It's God in our own smudged and diminished image.

In short, I've relinquished the transcendent God and transcendent humanity of my youth. (I mean *transcendent* in the misbegotten sense of being detached from Earth and nature.) Living Presence resides in, with, under, over, around, and beyond all that is. All is in God and God is in all.

I've also dropped the ancient question of why a good God permits evil. In a world of unparalleled human power, this version of the good-and-evil question points us in the wrong direction. The question for Anthropocene responsibility isn't why God permits evil; it's why we do. That's what Bonhoeffer and

Sittler were getting at: we need a faith and ethic coming of age for a world come of age.

Meanwhile, we have more to talk about in the next letter. It's about God and Albert Einstein.

Goodnight, Martín Theo.

Te amo,

Grandpa

THE UNCONTAINED GOD

Dear Martin Theo,

I've been reading Einstein. I'm surprised to hear so much God-talk since I had physicists pegged as agnostics and atheists. Another stereotype to drop.

Einstein rejected a personal God of rewards and punishments who intervened in life, and he had little time for rituals and authorities (including authorities of most any kind). He did align with Spinoza's God, which means he was forever attracted to the awe-inspiring beauty, rationality, and unity of nature's laws.

Einstein's cited often for what he said over and over: "God does not play dice with the universe." Things aren't random. Chance doesn't rule. And he always deflected the charge that he was an atheist: "There are people who say there is no God. But what makes me really angry is that they quote me for support of such views."

Einstein tapped into one of the great religious traditions— mysticism. Sometimes he identified it as such. Mystery, he said, was "the cradle of all true art and science," and a person "to whom this emotion is a stranger, who can no longer wonder and stand rapt in awe, is as good as dead, a snuffed-out candle." For him, being religious meant sensing something *beyond*, "something that our minds cannot grasp, whose beauty and sublimity reaches us only indirectly." In that sense of religion as mystery, he defined himself as "a devoutly religious man."

To say "that behind anything that can be experienced there is something that our minds cannot grasp" is to hint at an uncontained God. When we acknowledge there is something our minds cannot grasp, we realize God reaches us only on the slant. God arrives obliquely.

When he spoke at Union Seminary in 1940, Einstein said that science could be pursued only by people who aspired to understand the objective truth of material reality. The "source of feeling, however, springs from the sphere of religion." Yet it was Einstein's conclusion that made front-page news the next day: "The situation may be expressed by an image: science without religion is lame, religion without science is blind."

Why do I bring up Einstein? I'm not altogether sure, other than I'm fascinated with his God, his physics, and his metaphysics.

Look at subatomic, atomic, and molecular structure. Well, you can't look—atoms and molecules are so tiny they make itsy-bitsy seem obese.

But the beauty of science and technology is that they extend our senses.

They let me know that when I drink a glass of water, as I'm doing right now, a trillion trillion water molecules slide down my throat. And your next breath takes in a billion trillion molecules of air. The number of molecules in your body is roughly one followed by twenty-eight zeros. That's a million times the number of stars in the visible universe!

So little and unimaginably numerous! That's the substructure of everything everywhere and everywhen. "As little, so big," from the atom to the Milky Way and immensities beyond.

Why not put "as little, so big" on your backpack? Your friends might think "little" and "big" refer to you, and then you can tell them your molecules far outnumber the stars and have a good conversation about wonders.

Or you could talk about microbes.

Spud, do you remember from Eduardo's timeline when multicellular creatures developed? (We're that tribe.) Well, perhaps as many as fifty billion species of multicellular life have walked, flown, swum, burrowed, crawled, or waddled over the Earth. And the reason any life had a little Earth time is microbial activity and ingenuity. No wonder microbes are called "the little god." Even in your own body, microbial cells vastly outnumber the stars. And in your mouth alone, you have four hundred different *species* of microbes. They're a large part of "the zoo in you."

But back to Einstein. For him, the universe is matter and energy. Were that not wonder enough, many physicists now argue that the potential for the entire universe may be present at its origin. This includes the eventual emergence of intelligent life. As Freeman Dyson put it, "the universe in some sense must have known we were coming."

I think of it like this. Just as the architecture of every human being sits in every single human cell as DNA, so apparently in that infinitesimally small dot of Big Bang fame lay a "cosmic genome," so to speak, ready for the 13.8 billion-year journey (and counting).

But what most fascinates me about biological wonder, quantum physics, and cosmic consciousness is the unity of all that is through billions of years. It bespeaks a vast, if contained, universe and an uncontained God.

Religious traditions have long intuited this cosmic Presence. The language is that of spirit, spirit animating all. Here's a stanza of St. Patrick's Breastplate Hymn from the fifth century CE: "I bind to myself today, The energy of stars, The brilliance of sun, The whiteness of moon, The splendor of fire, The flashing of lightning, The wildness of wind, The depth of seas, The fecundity of earth, The solidity of rocks." But only recently has religion's flow of binding energy everywhere linked arm in arm with modern science as a companion.

I'm also fascinated that the vast quantity of cosmic energy is unseen. The "organized," visible energy that is matter—all those galaxies and their solar systems—occupies but a fraction of space, only 5 to 6 percent. The rest is not empty, however. There is no empty space. It's filled, brimming with dark matter and dark energy that, at this juncture, remains mysterious. Currently, scientists estimate that dark matter occupies 24 percent of all the stuff in the universe, and dark energy comes in at a whopping 70 percent.

And I'm fascinated that so many keywords about what is real yet nonvisible are highly "energetic" words—*spirit, soul, spirituality*, and *consciousness* itself. They exude nonvisible energy and name something important, if also mysterious.

The energy field that is everywhere has always been. As part of that, your atoms and mine scatter to become other things, just as those atoms existed before you and me and became us. I'm sure I've mentioned Joanna Macy before: "I just try to act my age. My atoms are 14 billion years old." Then there's Walt Whitman in the 1892 version of "Song of Myself": "For every atom belonging to me as good belongs to you."

Spud, for me this is very personal. I don't fear the moment of death; I fear dying. Death as no longer having a pulse counts far less than death as no longer being a self that relates and knows.

Now I'm digressing again. What I most want to voice is the wonder that washes over me as I contemplate belonging to all that is and to what so many have named your name, *Theos*.

None of this is scientific proof of God. It doesn't claim that and shouldn't be considered so. Instead, it's a meeting ground, almost a playground, for spirited discussion that ping-pongs back and forth between science and religion.

To Einstein again. Einstein never claims to know who or what God is *other than a presence manifest behind and in all things yet beyond our comprehension.*

He did reply to a sixth grader who asked him, "Do scientists pray?" After saying that a scientist would not be inclined to believe that events could be influenced by a supernatural being who intervenes in people's actions, he went on to affirm that "a spirit is manifest in the laws of the Universe—a spirit vastly superior to that of man, and one in the face of which we with our modest powers must feel humble. In this way the pursuit of science leads to a religious feeling of a special sort, which is indeed quite different from the religiosity of someone more naïve."

I'm joining Einstein on the limits of human knowing and on the felt presence of a cosmic spirit that includes our own spark but is vastly more.

We do violence to that presence when we sabotage the natural world. Human-induced degradation of Earth destroys swaths of God's presence. Degradation and extinction diminish God, stripping God of the manyness God requires *as* God. We wipe out whole patches of glory that shines everywhere.

Perhaps you've noticed the Orthodox icon in my office. The icon features three images. All are ancient: roiling waters as the waters of life, the Tree of Life at the center (as it is in Eden), and the sacred mountain divided so as to reveal an opening to Paradise. Above them, the dome is home to golden rays of sunshine and plentiful refreshing rain.

Gold calligraphy superimposed on the living waters identifies this icon as *The Incarnate God*.

Did you notice what's missing? Human beings, or indeed signs of any human presence whatsoever. No buildings, no fields, not even a well-traveled pathway. There is writing, however. It's Greek shorthand inscribed alongside the Tree of Life. The full identification reads in a note: "'Christ the Tree of Life,' by Father Andrew Tregubov, is an allegorical image of Paradise."

Take a moment to digest that: the universal Christ is not a human being here but a tree.

This icon was the centerpiece for an Orthodox Summit on the Environment in Baltimore in November of 1995. The public ritual at the summit was a blessing of the waters of Baltimore harbor after extensive port renovations and in celebration of the harbor's recovery from years of pollution. "The Incarnate God" symbolizes redeemed and flourishing creation and, doing what icons do, invites meditation on the living presence of this incarnate God.

True to Orthodox theology, redemption in this moment at the harbor is cosmic in scope. In contrast to Protestantism, the

Eastern church does not concentrate on sin but on deliverance from death and its corruption for the sake of flourishing creation. Furthermore, this is good news for *all* creatures, not just human beings. Indeed, in the central sacrament of every Orthodox Mass, the Eucharist, *all nature* is transfigured.

This good news notwithstanding, life is suffering too. It's public suffering and private, collective and individual, human and other-than-human together. Any God who does not face down reality on the home turf of death cannot meet us where the world is, in its terror as well as its beauty. Any God who does not know the worst from the inside out is not fully incarnate. Any God who does not know vulnerability, uncertainty, and despair cannot be the God of those who do. Only the One who has undergone all can overcome all.

I add that the reason I'm enamored, as Einstein was, with "the luminous figure of the Nazarene" is that Jesus enters the world's broken places to bring healing from the inside out. And no matter how forbidding the experience, he never gives up on *tikkun olam* (Hebrew for "repair of the world"). He lives the recklessness of God's dream to the bitter end.

Martín, this seems enough heavy lifting for one day! But I do have to add that my tragic view of human nature and history sits alongside a conviction that the existence of the world and universe is astonishing and life is a miracle—in fact, *the* miracle. I feel awe, mystery, and gratitude in the presence of all that is, seen and unseen. These feelings bring serenity and the embrace of grace. Thus does my tragic view of life partner with hope and a somewhat unexpected love of life. There's something rather than nothing, and it's alive everywhere. We belong to an uncontained God.

That presence will continue despite my skepticism that we have either the language or the minds for ultimate things. It will continue despite my conviction that we participate in Being with every breath we take and every thought we have but that God is not *a* being anywhere. Living Presence spills over the edges of our words, creeds, and deeds, and God-talk will continue as it has from the dawn of human time, from those first cave paintings, from the dedication of the first child in the moonlight to the Nameless One, and from the treasures buried with the dead in the first funerals. My hope is that God in the Anthropocene, Einstein's beloved *Alte* (Ancient One), is, as Bonhoeffer pleaded, God found in what we *do* know and *in our strengths and powers,* not simply in their absence and in our woeful ignorance. I'm hoping for a God that befits *sapiens* taking full human responsibility for what we know and do.

Goodnight, Martín Theo.

Te amo,

Grandpa

DEMOCRACY ENDANGERED

November 10, 2020

Dear Eduardo, dear Martín,

We know what you've been up to lately! Your folks sent a picture. You were on your way home in jackets with stickers that said *Future Voters,* each with a big checkmark. Your parents' stickers said *I Voted.*

This was your mom's first election as a US citizen! Do you remember when she went to be sworn in, Eduardo? You wanted to know if the judge explained American football to her since she shows zero interest. You also wondered whether the judge told her she should speak English from now on and not Spanish. (He didn't bring it up.)

What an inaugural election for your mom. This one is headed for the record books.

My own first election was in the Petersburg Town Hall. Shards of sunlight streamed through windows along the west wall to magnify the dust moving in that dim, musty room. Voting booths weren't booths at all, just a couple rows of small recycled desks from Petersburg Grade School.

I came home from college to cast my first ballot in 1960. The three-hour drive was a measure of its importance as a quiet rite of passage for me and my family. The outcome was Kennedy over Nixon in what turned out to be the closest election in presidential history to that point. We found out later that Kennedy's slim victory was indebted to Black voters.

I jump from that election to yours, Eduardo. I hear that within minutes after voting, you kept asking, "Did Biden win yet?" No answer was forthcoming for days, and you turned to more important things, like building Lego towers.

When the Associated Press finally called the election, a video has you hopping around the room, repeating "Biden won!" Only missing is the confetti. Spud is doing much the same, in full imitation of you. At two, he wasn't fully tuned in, however. "Wass-a-Biden," "Wass-a-Biden," he asked.

Your victory celebration was welcome comic relief for an election that leaves me more troubled than ever.

White identity politics was Trump's governing strategy. Election strategy too—white fear, white grievance, white nationalism, white privilege, and white supremacy. And he had enough charisma to embolden millions who felt forgotten. He cut a channel for the pent-up anger of those who felt they were losing their country. All of it added up to race-tinged patriotism among his core supporters.

This was white identity roused and put on defense. When white privilege is assumed, as mine was in Petersburg, it doesn't even surface. But when it feels menaced and under attack, it's a virulent force fighting the fear that a white-ruled America is ending. To fragile white privilege, even *talk* of equality feels like oppression. "Whiteness is a helluva drug," as a television commentator said recently.

Yet understanding Trump isn't my aim. I'm trying to fathom the loyalty of seventy-four million supporters and what it means for the nation. How will this election look in the rearview mirror?

Back in the 1960s, I gave no thought that irreconcilable divisions might threaten democracy itself. The struggles then—the civil rights movement, the protest against the Vietnam War, the early rustlings of feminism—were struggles for a more inclusive, more accountable democracy rather than the end of it. Voter registration, not voter suppression, was the campaign, and overturning election results wasn't on anyone's mind. The future felt open-ended, and we were more expectant than set on edge.

We were certainly not ready to buy and bear arms in record numbers, show up as militias at state capitols, and dance to the Second Amendment. It never occurred to me then that we could implode and end up a failed state. I still push hard against that thought. It creeps in anyway. A deeply polarized nation needs a cleansing. Otherwise democracy buckles.

Here's a conversation that haunts me. Isabel Wilkerson, author of *Caste*, was talking with Taylor Branch, an esteemed historian of the civil rights movement. Wilkerson wanted Branch's thoughts about white citizens' response to the prediction that by 2042, the United States will be a majority of racial minorities. (Eduardo, you'll be twenty-seven; Martín, you'll be twenty-four; both of you will have *I Voted* stickers.)

"People were angry when the predictions came out. People said they wouldn't stand for being a minority in their own country," Branch replied.

"Now there are troops at the border," Wilkerson added, "and shootings of black and brown and Jewish people." (This last reference came just days after the massacre at the Tree of Life Synagogue in Pittsburgh.)

Taylor nodded, thinking, and then asked, "So the real question would be . . . if people were given the choice between democracy and whiteness, how many would choose whiteness?"

Has it come to this, that most whites would rather live in a white authoritarian state than in a multiracial democracy in which they are a minority?

Let me think about this a bit longer. But not about the Trump years. By the time you take up your life work, they will have passed, presumably. I want to consider instead your future and the "cascading challenges" Biden says total the greatest threat this nation has known—climate change, the pandemic, gross inequality, racial injustice, abdication of global leadership, and attacks on the key institutions of democracy such as truth, trust, and elections.

The changes needed to meet this crisis of crises will have to be dramatic. Gradualism and incrementalism aren't enough. Increments don't move mountains, and gradualism doesn't reshape culture and institutions sufficiently fast. Without dramatic change, an ungovernable country is not beyond question.

The extreme case is collapse. I'll list factors you can use for your own test of the signs to watch for.

Joseph Tainter's *The Collapse of Complex Societies* (1988) was the initial account. "Civilizations are fragile, impermanent things," he wrote. Like empires, they cease to exist.

Tainter says collapse has two features. One is "the inexorable trend" of societies toward greater complexity, specialization, and control. Large, complex societies must be organized around formal structures that go well beyond kinship-based community. That means elaborate structures that command legitimacy and respect. And it means that trust in large institutions and collective actions must span multiple social groups. If pan-social trust is missing and cannot be reestablished, society collapses. Truth, trust, and transparency are requisites for complex societies striving to be democratic.

The diminishing returns of social complexity is the second feature. Greater and greater costs yield less and less.

To cite a real-world example of a civilization that collapsed under its own weight, Rome sacked its neighbors for more and more wealth. That in turn required more and more military presence and expanded, expensive bureaucracy, just to tread imperial waters. Collapse came when the empire overreached and sank from exhaustion. Goths and Visigoths (our genteel Swedish ancestors!) breached the barricades. (Incidentally, did you know that right now the United States has 750 military bases in eighty countries?)

Rome fell for other reasons, too, including economic depression and a plague. But the vulnerability that social complexity and turmoil generated seems uppermost. A disaster of some sort, even a major one—say, a climate event or a pandemic—doesn't of itself result in collapse, although disasters commonly expose society's fault lines. The collapse comes when society is unable to coordinate its response with sufficient means at sufficient scale to meet the larger-than-life challenges.

Does any of this sound familiar? It should, because we're living it. Once again, the wild card is us. Whether we'll succeed or fail rests with how we rally and deploy our powers in the face of large-scale vulnerabilities and amid uncertainty.

Tainter's account was followed by Jared Diamond's more extensive study of societies that crumbled. Diamond came to wonder why so many of the societies he studied fell. Most poignantly, why did they fall near the height of their power and numbers? And though their demise matured over an extended time, why did the fall seem sudden to those who suffered it? These questions led to his book *Collapse.*

Diamond has a formal definition. Collapse is an extreme form of decline that entails "a drastic decrease in human population size and/or political/economic/social complexity, over a considerable area, for an extended time."

Degraded environments are always *a* factor in collapse but not always the primary one. As *a* factor, Diamond identifies eight processes by which societies commit "unintended ecological suicide." These include deforestation, soil erosion, water shortages, overhunting, overfishing, the introduction of new species, human population growth, and the increased impact of people on the environment (read: carbon footprint and pollution).

To these eight, Diamond adds four new ones. They are new because they are modernity's fruit, most "abundant" in the Anthropocene: human-caused climate change, the buildup of toxic chemicals in the environment, energy shortages, and what he calls the full human utilization of the Earth's photosynthetic capacity. (Photosynthetic capacity is the maximum rate at which plants use sunlight to fix carbon. Diamond's point is that human-added greenhouse gases now exceed the planet's ability to deal with carbon dioxide.)

Diamond's worry is that most of these, if not all twelve, will be globally critical within the next few decades. (You too should count from 2005, when *Collapse* was published.) Either we solve the problems in this slim slice of time, or we face collapse.

Although you might expect Diamond's prognosis to be fatalistic, it isn't. Although he says we're looking at a future of increased pandemics and wars, lower living standards, and "the undermining of what we now consider some of our key values," Diamond's no determinist. He wants our collective moral choices made clear so that we scramble to overcome the inequities and degradation that lead to collapse. And he has at least one successful model of a society that's addressing reality—the Dutch. Not because they are morally exemplary people but because they realize that the whole world is a *polder*.

Polders are the below-sea-level lands the Dutch have been reclaiming for hundreds of years. Dutch wisdom says, "You have to be able to get along with your enemy, because he may be the person operating the neighboring pump in your polder." The person passing that along to Diamond goes on: "We're [now] all down in the polders together. It's not the case that rich people live safely up on the tops of the dikes while poor people live down in the polder bottoms below sea level. If the dikes and pumps fail, we'll all drown together." No bubble keeps anyone safe.

Differently said, the moral ecology of one-world dreamers now has a real-world counterpart. The planet you inherit, and that inherits you, is a polder. The Dutch know it up close and personal.

Overall, Diamond's account is scary because his succeed-or-fail choices set the bar so high. It's "love your neighbor or else." *Collapse* isn't too strong a word for what's coming if we don't change our ways.

But what's on my mind is specifically the threat to our democracy. We could have *both* national survival *and* the collapse of democracy. We could experience the kind of chaos that makes authoritarian leaders look like saviors, and we could, with them, survive in some undemocratic fashion.

Check your history books. Democracy's not the default position. Autocracy and plutocracy are more common and longer-lived. Autocracy is legal and political power largely in the hands of a single person (think monarchs and dictators). Plutocracy reigns when the wealthy wield all significant power. Amid historical options, democracy's a rare achievement.

The threat to democracy was seen when Trump refused in 2016 and 2020 to commit to the result of the vote ("I will tell you at the time . . . "). He leaned into autocracy and plutocracy. No surprise, then, that students of democracy have responded to Trumpian attacks with titles like *How Democracies Die, How Democracy Ends,* and *Democracy's Afterlife.*

Here's an important lesson from history: while civilization and barbarism aren't incompatible, democracy and demagoguery are.

Please know that this miserable note doesn't really match my usual mood. Your grandpa's not a curmudgeon. I'm a natural optimist who starts with the assumption that things will work out.

But things may not work out, your "Biden won!" notwithstanding. Bipartisan majority rule has been aberrant, including Biden's Obama years. If that continues, democracy moves into its afterlife.

Such realities never spring to life all of a sudden. If democracy dies, it will die of causes building for generations. Factors like the systemic inequality developing since the 1970s, the fraying of the social fabric and lack of attention to the common good in the Bush administration, and the centuries-long failure to systemically address race and caste. Then there's accumulating environmental degradation, biodiversity loss, the corruption of moneyed politics and the mistrust that grows with failed and costly wars. These factors all preceded Trump and will continue to poison life after him.

Most sobering is that these elements not only endanger democracy but belong to the corrosion that leads to collapse.

But let's look again at your mom's first election. The good news: Democracy's guardrails seem to have held. A fair, free, and disciplined election was served up. So there are reasons for optimism. Maybe that'll scatter these sad spirits. Hope so.

Carry on, you two, as will Grandma Nyla and I. We send bundles of love. Our favorite people call us Grandpa and Grandma.

Abrazos!

Grandpa

DEMOCRACY ENHANCED

January 18, 2021

Martin Luther King Day

Dear Martín and Eduardo,

The flag hangs at half-mast atop a darkened Capitol.
Who died?
Democracy.
Mobs breached Capitol security on January 6. For the first time in US history, there wasn't a peaceful transition from one president to the next as insurgents sought to stop Vice President Mike Pence and Republican and Democratic legislators from certifying the election of Joseph Biden and Kamala Harris.

Not long after, Donald Trump became the first president to be twice impeached, this second time for instigating insurrection. Thousands marched to the Capitol at his urging.

Not only Washington was in view. State capitols were as well. Your Grandma Nyla went to work at our capitol today behind barricades everywhere (she handles phone calls to legislators). Because of heightened security, she must use a single, strictly monitored entrance and exit. I can't drop her off there, however. Security allows no vehicles near the capitol, so she walks a block under police surveillance, all because of the insurrection.

Because the occupation of "the People's House" is certain to be in your history books, I'm skipping the details except to say that when I finished writing you shortly after Election Day, I regretted that I had dumped so much foreboding on you with so much talk of collapse. But I couldn't have imagined then what came to pass—a darkened, barricaded Capitol. Democracy's more endangered than I thought.

I intended to write you today about democracy and power, not insurrection, simply because your years are stamped by nothing so much as unprecedented human power and its spinoffs. How will Anthropocene reality be governed?

That the nation and world may be ungovernable returned me to Martin Luther King's struggle for expanded and enhanced democracy. Whether that vision can meet the challenges you face I don't know, but I want to find out.

King's campaign lodges in public memory as the civil rights movement. While not wrong, it's incomplete. You'll have seen footage of the March on Washington and heard the "I Have a Dream" speech. But it was not the March on Washington for Civil Rights. It was the March on Washington *for Jobs and Freedom*.

King's conviction was unwavering that genuine democracy— freedom—is economic, political, and social, each dimension critical for the others. The three together, equally for all, is democracy fulfilled.

The flag at half-mast also sends me to Reinhold Niebuhr. His writings on democracy merit another look, given the insurrectionists' insistence that they are true patriots who will fight for their country by any means necessary.

By the time Nyla and I arrived in New York in 1965, a series of small strokes had caused Niebuhr to set aside his busy schedule at Union. Nonetheless, he still held a seminar in the Niebuhr apartment on Riverside Drive. I took the one on Moral Norms in International Relations. More important to me, however, were weekly walks. Ursula Niebuhr, ever in banter mode, told us students, "It's quite enough that I have to walk Winnie (their standard poodle named for Winston Churchill). I can't be walking Reinhold too." So we students walked Reinhold, or Reinie, as both students and faculty called him.

Niebuhr wrote and thought a great deal about power: its uses, its abuses, its possible restraints. He was correct about many things, including the tendency of the powerful to resist any checks on their power. "There is no ethical force strong enough to place inner checks upon the use of power if its quantity is inordinate," he cautioned. Here as elsewhere, Frederick Douglass's point, made in 1857, stands: "Power concede[s] nothing without a demand. It never did and it never will." (Case in point: neither moral appeal nor logic had any effect whatsoever in altering the course of the aggrieved masses on January 6.)

Niebuhr also taught that evil and injustice flow from imbalances of power. Abuse of power follows from its concentration. This holds for every ideology, every period of history, and every human tribe from the family to the community of nations. Stab a page with your index finger in any of your history books and you'll find injustice flowing from imbalances of power.

This propensity to injustice on the part of the reigning powers usually put Niebuhr and King on the side of the underdog.

Both believed that the powerless had more of a right to fight for their violated rights than those already entrenched in powerful positions had a right to extend theirs.

It's not always obvious who is in power. In fact, those in power often prefer it that way, keeping their privilege under the radar, invisible even to themselves. They are self-deluded in their belief that they are the ones embodying law and order. This makes their privilege appear on the surface like nonviolence since they're not the agitators. They see overt opposition to their privilege as "a power move" on the part of dissidents, while their own habits are regarded as forces for stability and tranquility. Institutionalized privilege thereby appears "natural" and normative, while the ways of dissidents appear deviant, disruptive, and abnormal. This always places those trying to eliminate injustice "at the moral disadvantage of imperiling the peace."

This is why democracy and democratic power are so very precious. They act as a check on human beings' regular, even predictable, grabs for power while also giving us a matrix for achieving a common good. Democracy is not, for Niebuhr or King, the vote plus maximal liberty married to corporate-regulated markets in the interests of an ownership society represented by concentrated wealth. That kind of system "in which the fortunate few dominate the rest" is plutocracy, not democracy. Democracy is power that's accountable and equitably distributed. All this validates both clauses of Niebuhr's famous defense of democracy: "Man's capacity for justice makes democracy possible; man's inclination to injustice makes democracy necessary."

Yet Niebuhr also said that powerful democracies tend toward naïveté and self-delusion. The very idealism that bolsters the case for their existence as democracies can serve "innocently" to justify their imperialism. This was on display when President George W. Bush said that the United States' global mission on behalf of freedom was not imperial and ought never be viewed in that way. War was justified because America would bring democracy to Iraq and Afghanistan.

Unfortunately, religion too often plays along, intensifying the underlying power dynamics. Yes, religious *humility* tends to hold power accountable to norms beyond itself as we are judged by transcendent standards not of our own making. On the other hand, religious *pride* tends to foster extremism, fanaticism, intolerance, exclusivism, and absolutism. "Religion is humility before the absolute and self-assertion in terms of the absolute," Niebuhr said in a fine statement of human nature, home to good twinned with evil. (The Proud Boys, along with other far-right militia groups assaulting the Capitol on January 6, raised money for the insurrection on Christian nationalist websites.)

Niebuhr later nuanced his thesis on religion with attention to a third factor, religious indifference. He did so as modern secular culture grew increasingly indifferent toward historic forms of religious faith.

That indifference brought a liberal tolerance welcomed by both Niebuhr and King. But for them liberal tolerance is too shallow to keep society together. It doesn't provide a common memory, history, focus, purpose, or meaning. It doesn't generate love or community. Boys, neither religious indifference nor tolerance will provide the Anthropocene communities of character you will need: stable, ongoing associations of persons with commitments to one another, a shared experience of life together, and joint purpose.

I'm thinking of the motto in shiny brass at the United Church of Santa Fe: "Love God, Love Neighbor, Love Creation." Something would be lost if it were "Tolerate God, Tolerate Neighbor, Tolerate Creation"!

Niebuhr and King on power, all well and good. But there's still the "so what?" question. What's their capacity to guide us now—and you in the future?

Niebuhr's wisdom about human nature and power led him to lay out, in 1932, the fundamentals of what became the civil rights movement, decades before struggles took on segregated lunch counters, schools, and state capitols. There are lessons here you can tap.

In his realism about the nature of power, he wrote that while there would be "a number of individual white men . . . who will identify themselves completely with the Negro cause, *the white race in America will not admit the Negro to equal rights if it is not forced to do so. Upon that point one may speak with a dogmatism which all history justifies.*" In writing this, he echoes Frederick Douglass in power conceding nothing apart from countervailing power.

For Niebuhr, realism means it is hopeless to depend on "the moral sense of the white race" while holding that "it is equally hopeless to attempt emancipation through violent rebellion." Where whites hold prevailing power and the will to use it, they will use it.

After he entertains forms of gradualism, he sees that such efforts "operate within a given system of injustice . . . [and] don't make a frontal attack upon the social injustices from which the Negro suffers." The alternative he then lays out is "non-violent coercion and resistance."

Nonviolence is clearly a form of coercion, and coercion is necessary in Niebuhr's eyes and King's. But it's a type of coercion that allows the adjustment of conflicting interests without destroying the moral force behind them. Today it's often called "soft power" to contrast it with harsh, no-give domination.

Niebuhr saw this soft power in workers' unionizing efforts as a way of getting to "yes" for all parties. And he conceived it as effective for African American struggles as well. Nonviolent power is, he pointed out, "a particularly strategic instrument for an oppressed group which is hopelessly in the minority and has no possibility of developing sufficient power to set against its oppressors."

Among the tactics he lists for nonviolent resistance are "Boycotts against banks which discriminate against Negroes in granting credit, against stores which refuse to employ Negroes while serving Negro trade, . . . Non-payment of taxes against states which spend on the education of Negro children only a fraction of the amount spent on white children, might be an equally efficacious weapon."

Niebuhr also speaks to ways in which religion usually intensifies power dynamics. Here Niebuhr says that there is "no problem of political life to which religious imagination can make a larger contribution than this problem of developing non-violent resistance." Exactly that contribution was core to the civil rights/enhanced democracy struggle, anchored as it was in the predominantly Black churches and their religious allies, Jews above all.

You'll recall our discussion of prophetic love and Rabbi Heschel. Heschel was a classic icon of the Selma march as, in full beard, long wavy gray hair, and looking for all the world like a Hebrew prophet, he marched arm in arm with Dr. King across the Edmund Pettus Bridge toward the Alabama state troopers. ("My legs were praying," Heschel said.) There is no accounting for the movement's successes, risks, and sacrifices apart from its mobilization of religious and spiritual power.

Let's hear from King and Niebuhr one last time.

I remember few of my afternoon talks with Niebuhr. I recall more vividly the times with King—in Riverside Church for his "Time to Break Silence" speech linking civil rights struggles to poverty and opposition to the Vietnam War. Then exactly a year later, on April 4, a lecture I attended at Riverside was interrupted to announce his assassination.

It was stupid of me not to keep a diary of the hours with Niebuhr and the times in King's presence. But I didn't.

One conversation does come to mind, however, aided no doubt by the effort this summer of 2020 and winter of 2021 to finally achieve a breakthrough in reckoning with white racism. Niebuhr had just come from a talk show where he and James Baldwin debated race matters. This must have been 1967, after the Voting Rights Act (1965) and Civil Rights Act (1966) had been signed. Yet King's campaign for economic equality, essential to enhanced democracy, was considered a bridge too far. As the *New Yorker* commented about his move North and his plans for a Poor People's Campaign in Washington, "King had begun to perceive that society tends to confine its indignation to injustices that can be attenuated without imperiling fundamental economic relationships."

On our walk, Niebuhr's pace quickened. He was clearly animated about the time with Baldwin. "We may actually clear this hurdle [of race] in a hundred years," he said, looking straight ahead. I don't recall my exact response beyond exclaiming *"one hundred years!"* For students in the 1960s, that timeline was ice water thrown on our idealism. We were confident we could best any battles in our own lifetime.

Only later did I learn Baldwin's view. In 1962, he said that the upcoming centennial celebration of the Emancipation Proclamation in 1965 would probably arrive "one hundred years too soon. We [Negroes] cannot be free until [whites] are free."

One hundred years. Both Baldwin and Niebuhr fore-saw another century of protracted struggle. They knew what I and my colleagues didn't—pandemics that have deep roots and institutional legs, like the pandemic of racism, take a long time to eradicate. Victories come by fits and starts and contests have to be engaged anew, over and again, not least because the poisonous virus develops new variant strains. This means you should celebrate victories when you can, rest up, return to the struggle with vigor, and pass the torch when you must.

Niebuhr had shortcomings. He never confronted eco-nomic injustice with the consistency King did. Nor, for all his insight on whites and race, was Niebuhr as consistently opposed to racial injustice as King. He sometimes joined those who found King moving too fast in efforts to upend white rac-ism. While King grew more radical year by year, Niebuhr grew less. In retrospect, and with a view to democracy now so endan-gered, King had the better grip.

In any case, I hope you and your friends attend carefully to Niebuhr and King on the dynamics of morality and power in human relationships. I cannot recall a moment when the moral-ity of power and the power of morality mattered more.

One gap in Niebuhr and King on power must be mentioned. They wrote relatively little about the vast exercise of power in the natural world. That's power as energy and capacity. It's power as "power to," and it's present in every atom, cell, body, planet, solar system, and galaxy. It's elemental and omnipresent, indispensable and universal. Nothing happens apart from power as power to. Nothing can. You will need to go elsewhere, then, to understand the millions of ordinary exchanges of power as energy, power operating as trillions of microorganisms in ecosystems and the multitudes in your own bodies. The wisdom of eco-womanists, eco-feminists, and Indigenous peoples is your go-to source for understanding natural world power merged with human power. There's your clue for Anthropocene living.

In other words, Niebuhr and King rarely extended their insights on power to ranks other than *sapiens*. In an epoch like yours, when *sapiens* reign everywhere for better and for worse, that becomes a serious oversight. How human power interacts with the rest of nature's is utterly consequential. To continue Holocene dualism is deadly.

These shortcomings acknowledged, make Niebuhr's wisdom and King's your own because you will, again and again, face social conflict trailing climate disruption, another pandemic, and we/they tribalism on a diminished planet. The insurrection of January 6 won't be the end of grievance politics, either. You don't want to be powerless in the face of such tumult. And the alternative of buying an arsenal and taking up arms, as was done by some for the insurrection, is patently absurd. Rescue, order, and peace will come by orchestrated cooperation, not pitched battle. So unless you have miraculously arrived at "liberty and justice for all," strategic nonviolence is your best choice of available powers. Love, healthy bodies, and friendship too. Above all, you will need to attend to power and its messiness in all forms.

It's time to close. Despite my sober words, I'm easily contented this evening. To cite a cartoon in my office, all I need is "a warm bed, a kind word, and unlimited power."

Los amo,

Grandpa

AFTERTIME

September 11, 2020

Dear Eduardo and Martín,

What a week! The Labor Day temperature in Santa Fe was 93° F, handily besting the record of 89°. Two days later, we awoke to the earliest snow matched to the coldest night, 31°. If you go from the high to the low, that's a swing of 62° in forty-eight hours.

State scientists are puzzling about a bird die-off we've been experiencing. Hypothermia is suspected—the birds couldn't keep warm enough. Why? The preliminary answer is that our sustained drought robbed them of adequate food (insects, seeds) and of water. Thus they lacked the reserve energy to fluff up their feathers when the cold snap came. Fluff-up is a way to keep warm.

And sure enough, Nyla and I noted several things. The birds are markedly more slender this year. We've gone through far more birdseed this summer—a normal week's supply disappears in two days, as though there were a drain. That's hunger. Birdbath visits are more numerous, too, but not for baths. They come to drink. That's thirst.

As scientists perform autopsies of the birds, they add new knowledge to their original hunches. In a single night the sudden cold snap killed off a major food supply—insects. That happens in winter, too, but not this suddenly and not this early, with no time to adjust. Further, the birds might still have survived this—and the majority did—had they not already been stricken by both drought and wildfires. The fires burned large areas of bird habitat and food sources, especially those migrating through California, Arizona, and Colorado. Because none of the birds had fat stores in their bodies, they were more susceptible to sudden hypothermia.

The larger picture is this. Roughly a quarter of the birds in the Western Hemisphere have disappeared in the last fifty years. In New Mexico, that ramps up to 80 percent for some critical species, like our piñon jay, which is the primary disperser of seeds for piñon pines. A die-off of jays means fewer piñon trees. Fewer trees likely means fewer birds and thinner forests. This is biodiversity's downward spiral.

One lesson is that we can't readily anticipate the ripple effects of fickle system change. In this case, the combination of drought, wildfire, and temperature extremes killed off the more vulnerable birds as they faced diminished food, water, habitat, and changed air currents. Yet no one saw this coming just a few days ago.

Even more unsettling is that, although what we know about climate system change is bad, what we don't know is likely much worse. Climate systems are huge, nonlinear, profoundly interactive, and deeply interconnected. The consequences of change to any one system can trail far into the future and affect others. So when system change runs to extremes, far more is set in motion than meets the present eye or past experience.

Look at the changed personality of recent hurricanes. Hurricanes now carry more moisture from warming waters, slow more when making landfall, and dump more rain for more days.

They grow stronger and move farther inland more often. Moreover, many have been forming closer to land, bedeviling evacuation efforts in coastal cities. Some are shifting poleward as well. (We caught the tail end of one in northwestern Scotland. Scotland's not hurricane territory.) Not least, warming ocean waters extend the hurricane season.

Fires have also morphed. Fire sizes are now "mega," and fire locations, fire frequency, and fire seasons are all on the move. Some fires are so large and intense that their blistering heat disrupts the atmosphere in ways that create their own weather. Droughts, too, lengthen and grow more severe even while some locations shift dramatically. Siberia and the Arctic both experience what only sci-fi imaginations entertained—drought and fire—as well as that oxymoron "thawing permafrost." Add rising seas and changed weather created by polar warming running four times the global average, and you inherit a different planet. Poets will mourn.

The marks of your young epoch where we've spilled the most ink are climate volatility, eco-social uncertainty, and mass extinction. Of these, you've likely studied climate volatility and eco-social uncertainty in school. But what about mass extinction? I did write about it earlier but didn't say that the biomass of our species and our livestock account for 96 percent of land mammal biomass. Nor did I say that only 3 percent of Earth's terrestrial ecosystems are free of human activity. This overcrowding by *sapiens* places "one in four species are at risk of extinction," says a PBS report that aired last evening. The same report notes that more than half of Earth's wildlife has disappeared in fifty years (two-thirds of your grandparents' lifetime and all of your dad's). Yet nothing appeared in today's papers. We have the attention span of a gnat—a little buzz and quickly out of sight. Like species extinction itself.

The cause of extinction is the devastating relationship to nature of our extractive, growth-obsessed economy. Our economic default is the fault itself. And the bottom line is that the natural world, including us, cannot be saved without working out a harmony of economy and ecology that still eludes us.

Sorry to be so glum this morning! It's a lousy way to start your day and mine. But I don't see how any of the good things around us become more abundant these coming decades. Quite the contrary—the tilt is downward.

Begin Again is Eddie Glaude Jr.'s book about James Baldwin. It's Baldwin with a purpose that's teed up in the subtitle: *James Baldwin's America and Its Urgent Lessons for Our Own.*

Glaude's striking phrase is "the after time." Borrowed from Walt Whitman's *Democratic Vistas* (1871), the after time follows the fury of the Civil War as a different nation emerges from the ashes. For Whitman, the new nation, whatever its character, does well not to forget the rage and fury. They remain a warning for postwar America because history doesn't really go away. There can be relapses, and the Civil War might not be over. History's not laid out end-to-end; it's stacked.

Glaude uses Whitman's "after time" for both the "disruption and splintering of the old ways of living" and "the making of a new community after the fall." The after time is thus in between, filled with perplexity about "what has gone before and what is coming into view." The nation doesn't quite know what it is; its narrative is muddled by its trauma.

For a little fun, let's merge the words to make *aftertime*. You remember that we talked about your playfulness with language, Eduardo, when you were reading words backward.

Baldwin lived through the tail end of one aftertime and the beginning of another. The first included the rise of Jim Crow, which was still in full swing when Baldwin was born in 1924. The Confederacy lost the Civil War in 1865 but won the peace in a backhanded way. Slavery didn't survive, but white supremacy did, in both the South and the North. "Created equal" didn't apply to "all men." A land of democracy, equality, and justice was the big lie white Americans believed and Black Americans were supposed to, despite daily evidence to the contrary.

Baldwin's second aftertime was the collapse of the civil rights movement. Assassinations took three of his good friends—Medgar Evers, Martin Luther King Jr., and Malcolm X—plus Robert Kennedy. These, together with the rise of Black Power, left Baldwin shaken.

But the truly tragic "after" of this aftertime was white America turning away yet again from any real change that would set the country right, any new way of keeping the promises made with every Pledge of Allegiance. Despite notable gains like the Voting Rights Act of 1965, the country managed "to stay true to the inequalities of the American story." So Baldwin found himself with a second national betrayal. He gave up on white America saving itself and on white America being saved by Black America. All must be saved together or not at all for Baldwin. His love of country and the tenacity of a New Jerusalem never let go, though he left the United States for what Glaude calls his "elsewheres" in Paris and Istanbul.

Baldwin did not live to see the country saved. He died in 1987. (I was at his memorial service. Ask me about it sometime.) With his death, his aftertime question was left hanging: what sort of people, finally, do we take ourselves to be?

We're living in a third aftertime, with the rise of Black Lives Matter and, for the first time, the interrogation of white supremacy by whites. My question is whether this third aftertime will become the third betrayal. Is the corner turned, or is another failed reckoning in the offing?

Baldwin's are not your only aftertimes. I started this letter with the bizarre climate of early September. But note that the letter's date is the nineteenth anniversary of 9/11. With the exception of bloody Brits ransacking the Capitol in 1812, the nation had never been attacked by foreign terrorists on its own soil. On September 11, 2001, commercial carriers were flown as bombs into the World Trade Center, the Pentagon, and, on a plane bound for the Capitol, into a field in Pennsylvania. (Passengers wrested the plane from the terrorist pilots but could not control it. Everyone perished.)

This aftertime is a terrorist time. More carefully said, a time when terrorism leaves marks on an age and feels like disease or trauma.

These analogies are not precise, I know. I mean only to say that now we don't live without terrorism resting somewhere in our psyche. We confront new levels of vulnerability. That's our aftertime. Not enough to keep us awake but enough to keep us anxious.

Nyla and I lived at 122nd and Broadway on 9/11. We had both gone off to work that fall morning of azure skies and bright sun, she to New York Hospital on the East Side, I across the street to Union. Nancie Erhard, a friend and PhD student, had come from Nova Scotia to meet me for a session on her dissertation draft. We were in the coffee shop when a staff person came to say, "Larry, I think you'd better go to the TV in the student lounge. A plane just crashed into the World Trade Center." Since Nancie was to catch her flight home after our meeting, I said, "Let's finish our discussion then check the TV." We suspected a tragic accident. Terrorism as a mindset wasn't yet sufficiently in place to warn us otherwise.

The rest of the morning is vague to me. I suppose I was glued to television in the student lounge and at home. Your dad called from grad school in Champaign-Urbana to check on us. East Berlin friends called too.

At Union, I gathered with others in James Chapel, drawn by a force we couldn't resist. Whether someone led a formally structured time I don't recall. It was the first week of classes, and I do remember an entering student, Melanie Harris, singing our lamentations with such power that tears flowed freely among many, like me, trying to hold them back. I also recall another new student clutching her flip phone and then stepping out into the entryway when it rang, only to return shouting, "He's alive! My husband's OK! Thank God!" He worked on the World Trade Center plaza.

Nyla and I have often mused about the aftertime of 9/11. Unlike others, including the civil rights movement, it suffers notable absences. Why is there is no Ground Zero psalm or a Manhattan prayer for the ages?

There is a very moving memorial at the footprint of each tower, however. One peers over the low perimeter to watch water falling into a darkening abyss with no bottom. Sounds of silence are the only ones you hear. It's as though grief and trauma haven't yet found their voice. Except in the name given the bottomless pools—*Reflecting Absence*.

In the days after 9/11, I gave an address on "The American Way in the Presence of Fear" and came across prophetic words from *New Yorker* writer E. B. White. White wrote a reflection on the vulnerability of modern cities in 1948 for a little book, *Here Is New York:*

> The subtlest change in New York is something people don't speak much about but that is in everyone's mind. The city, for the first time in its long history, is destructible. A single flight of planes no bigger than a wedge of geese can quickly end this island fantasy, burn the towers, crumble the bridges, turn the underground passages into lethal chambers, cremate the millions. The intimation of mortality is part of New York now. . . . It used to be that the Statue of Liberty was the signpost that proclaimed New York and translated it for all the world. Today Liberty shares the role with Death.

White was on to something: Our aftertimes are about vulnerability, especially collectively. In Toni Morrison's words, "the destiny of the twenty-first century will be shaped by the possibility or the collapse of a shareable world." That world is where Grandma Nyla, I, and you two are.

The corona universe has been so much a part of your lives to date, and our letters, that it asks no more than honorable mention as your aftertime. Nonetheless, it, too, is a mass-casualty event. The virus death toll will likely be in the millions worldwide. And while vaccines will arrive before long, the economic, health, social, and cultural effects of the pandemic will linger.

This may sound improbable—it startles me—but you two have still another aftertime, and it surpasses Baldwin's, 9/11, and the pandemic. It's where this letter started, with Earth signaling that we've fallen off the back end of the reliable Holocene into the volatile Anthropocene.

A few years ago, I never would have guessed your aftertime would bridge the moat between geological epochs. You'll be creating a different way of life than your grandparents.'

Where you do that, and with whom, matters. As you practice the future, attend to who's on your left and right, who's in front and who's behind. The company you keep makes all the difference.

Los amo,

Grandpa

ELSEWHERE

September 15, 2020

Dear Eduardo and Martín,

Baldwin moving away to Paris sparked my interest in "elsewheres." What might elsewhere mean for you if you experience convulsive years? *Haven* is the word that crosses my forehead like tickertape in Times Square—*haven . . . haven . . . haven*. Lifesaving havens may be as necessary for you as the food, drink, music, and friendship I hope are part of them.

Elsewhere may truly be somewhere else—a different address, a different culture. For Baldwin, it was Paris and Istanbul, far from Harlem and America. He needed those havens for his sanity. While Baldwin did his most famous writing there, he cast off to those places to ponder being Black in America, not Black in Paris or Black in Istanbul. To be present to his own reality, he had to get away.

I remember Nyla and I helping Manas and Grace Buthelezi get settled in our Washington, DC, neighborhood. Manas was deeply immersed in anti-apartheid struggles in South Africa, and I suspected he and his family left because of threats against them. But when I asked why he accepted a year's teaching in DC, his reply was "to think about South Africa." In the midst of all-consuming struggles, and amid danger, people sometimes need to make landfall far enough away for rest, reflection, and renewal.

I'm wondering where your elsewhere might be. Perhaps Colombia with your mom's family—your *abuelos*, if they are still alive by the time you read these letters, and all those spirited aunts, uncles, and cousins. Medellín is already a kind of second home for you.

My elsewhere was Berlin, starting in 1963–64, with five friends.

The year 1963 turned out to be traumatic for Americans. Yet I didn't go to Berlin with Baldwin's purpose in mind, seeking a way to consciously confront America and its betrayals. As we disembarked our ship at Bremerhaven, who we were as a nation was not on our minds at all. Polishing our German language skills was, exploring Berlin was, new adventures were.

We arrived in the late summer of 1963, shortly after President Kennedy's visit in June. The air was still charged, and everyone had tales of his visit they wanted us to hear. In no time at all, we realized that Berliners were talking as though we, too, had been dusted with the Kennedy magic, just as they had.

On November 22 Kennedy was assassinated. As the American working in a neighborhood center that had been a refugee camp before the Wall, so many flowers and cards of condolence came my way that we had no more room for them. Not that those good folks were strangers. Although only months into our year together, I already knew most of them as regulars who came for lunch daily and stayed for games, conversation, and *kaffee und kuchen* at 4:00 p.m. Most were elderly refugees who, unlike young people, did not want to be relocated to West Germany. They clung to their hope that the Wall wouldn't stand and they would soon see family and friends again in the East. (The Wall fell on November 9, 1989, after most of them had died.)

As refugees, they couldn't cross to the East at Checkpoint Charlie, no matter the reason and the short distance. But as an American in a city under four-power rule (Britain, France, the United States, and the USSR), I could, so I made trips on their behalf. Sometimes it was to take news and get news—weddings, graduations, memorial services. Sometimes it was to deliver requested medicines I had to smuggle in. And sometimes it was to clandestinely carry, usually in my underwear, a TV part that let their families watch West TV on the sly. I was never caught, except for other contraband, mostly forbidden books scattered "naively" among others in a box easily opened.

The flowers, cards, and remembrances I received after Kennedy's assassination were deeply moving. Equally so was nighttime on November 22 and 23 at the Wall, which was close to where I lived. At dusk, a candle appeared in what seemed every window in the East, lit in memory of President Kennedy. The candlelight met darkness as apartment lights were extinguished. Though burning a candle for hours was surely an act of courage—addresses could easily be known by police and spying neighbors—I doubt any held back. For many, a yearning for freedom likely flickered in those flames. But for us the sculpted memory was their affection for our idealistic young president.

Thanksgiving was hard. Where would we, four days after Kennedy was killed, celebrate it? And with whom?

Grace came by way of the Heichlers. Lucian Heichler was the American diplomat attached to the office of Berlin's mayor, Willy Brandt. As such, Lucian was cohost to Kennedy for his visit. Now, but days after the assassination, Lucian and Muriel Heichler invited us and other Americans to a Thanksgiving table that reached across two large rooms in their spacious home. I don't remember Lucian's remarks, but I still feel the emotions they evoked. And I remember long evening and Sunday afternoon talks about being Americans in a nation that often assassinates its best leaders. Berlin was our elsewhere, a time and place to take stock and make sense of it all, if sense could be made. We cherished our friendship—it's sustained us since—but the year was steeped in both euphoria and despondency.

The same can be said for 1968–69, when I returned to Berlin for the year, this time with Nyla. The spring and summer of '68 at home was shock and trauma. Dr. King was assassinated April 4 and Robert Kennedy June 6. I felt nothing but relief as we boarded for the crossing that summer. I wanted to be elsewhere.

Not that elsewhere needs to be abroad. My favorite poet and theologian is Maya Angelou. ("Theologian" is my designation, not hers.) Born Marguerite Annie Johnson in St. Louis on April 4, 1928, her older brother nicknamed her Maya, as in "my-a sister," and she kept that when she later changed her birth name. What she called her parents' "calamitous marriage" found her at age three, and her brother at four, sent off to their grandmother in Stamps, Arkansas. Stamps, Arkansas, was full-on Jim Crow.

At age twelve she returned to St. Louis and was raped by her mother's boyfriend. Maya went mute for almost five years, until she was seventeen.

That was her traumatic elsewhere-in-place. Smothered in silence and solitude, she dove into books, developed an extraordinary memory, and cultivated remarkable gifts for observing everything offered by two worlds, the one around her and the other in her imagination. When her speech returned at seventeen, she was sent to her grandmother again and, it turns out, to her grandmother's friend Mrs. Bertha Flowers. Bertha took Maya in hand and introduced her to Shakespeare, Charles Dickens, Edgar Allen Poe, James Weldon Johnson, and Georgia Douglas Johnson. The poet, extraordinary wordsmith, and memoirist was born. (You can read her account in *I Know Why the Caged Bird Sings*.)

Eventually she traveled abroad. In Paris she met James Baldwin, and he became "my brother." Back in the States, in Harlem, she became a friend of Malcolm X and worked as an organizer for Dr. King. (She turned forty the day he was assassinated.)

What a strange elsewhere-in-place her mute years had been. In what must be the most extreme of ironies, that teen trauma was the strange, unwanted, and perverse "haven" where she honed the gifts that made her the extraordinary person she was. Someday you two should do yourselves the favor of sitting quietly with *On the Pulse of Morning*, the poem she wrote for the 1992 presidential inauguration. It is unsurpassed in providing the language and vision of what the world has been over eons and might yet be.

Her vision is a pretty good summation of the necessary onset for undertaking your roles in that world to come. Your tasks are framed by the fact that you're Anthropocene kids. That means, in Angelou's words, you have "no hiding place." Climate collapse and pandemics mean that security zones are gone. Nature changing course dramatically is an aftertime your elsewheres cannot escape.

This is why I hope you have havens. They are more important than ever, even when they cannot be on a different planet than the one that's webbed in frightening degree. Though this sounds bleak, I'm just being honest. The world is "too dangerous for anything but truth and too small for anything but love," to recall William Sloane Coffin.

Yet honesty about Earth's anger only detracts momentarily from the exhilarating work before you and the chariots of fire you'll ride. The big challenges will galvanize your calling.

The cultural historian Thomas Berry knows your challenges and promise as well as anyone. Every civilization and people have a "Great Work," he says, from the humanism of ancient Greece to Israel's experience of the divine in human affairs, Western Europe's soaring cathedrals, and the Great Work of the First Peoples in America, establishing an intimate rapport with the powers that brought this continent into existence. These are splendid examples of how the same, shared human nature generated very different cultures, some of them exquisite.

And your own Great Work? It's to effect "the transition from a period of human devastation of the Earth to a period when humans [are] present to the planet in a mutually beneficial manner." A "technozoic" era becomes an "ecozoic" one.

The ecozoic is both journey and goal. That's your aftertime. It's how you become good ancestors. Havens will be part of it.

I'm eager for our next letters. None is short on love.

Los amo,

Grandpa

RESPONSIBLE BY DEGREES

Dear Martín, dear Eduardo,

I had imagined these letters as a cascade of stories, a few reflections on your lives and ours, and some humor. Instead, they turned somber as I've tried to say how your years look for the planet you inherit.

That has shoved certain questions front and center, landing there because your lives and ours are home to different epochs. In several letters, the lead question has been the difference it makes if the human condition is the same—or not. Does it matter that you are Anthropocene kids and Grandma Nyla and I are Holocene kids? If so, how?

We'll eventually finish this line of questioning—don't give up hope!—by outlining what's most important for you and everyone else: renewed human responsibility.

What makes another look necessary is that we now wield powers once reserved for the gods. As Stewart Brand put it in 1968, "We are as gods and might as well get good at it." Later he was more emphatic: "We are as gods and *have to* get good at it." *Homo deus*—the god species—is who we've become.

We're named as such by Big History writers like Yuval Noah Harari, who says that until recently, evolution has followed the unchanging principles of natural selection. Now, however, "humankind is poised to replace natural selection with intelligent design."

Intelligent? Maybe in the future, but so far design has been too happenstance and without conscious, shared intention. Planetary ecosystems are "managed" more as a consequence of an assumed way of life and powerful technologies than deliberation. That's more accident than design and not very intelligent.

Biologist E. O. Wilson is even more skeptical: "We are not as gods. We're not yet sentient or intelligent enough to be much of anything." (Spud, do you remember Richard Leakey's remark that we're the only species he knows that consistently makes bad decisions?)

But Harari is correct that our powers *do* take the evolutionary process beyond natural selection, and any account of responsibility is truthful only if it confronts our powers on this novel scale in these novel ways.

Assisted evolution is the going term for what we're doing. But it's deceptive because it hides the depth and breadth of the evolutionary changes we're effecting. Would you have guessed from *assisted evolution* that our extra carbon would remake the world, alter marine chemistry, flood coastlines, strip glaciers "to bare bones," embolden deserts, warp the circulation of ocean currents, "supercharge extreme weather events," and rearrange "the distribution of animal, plant, and microbial species across the globe"? Would you have guessed that every major taxonomic group—animals, insects, plants, fungi, and microorganisms—is being driven down new evolutionary paths by human-assisted changes? *Assisted evolution* is room-temperature talk that doesn't begin to reveal what we've done; we've created "no-analog climates, no-analog ecosystems, a whole no-analog future." *Hijacked and hacked evolution* would be more honest.

The stakes of a human-dominated no-analog world are stark. If *Homo dominatus* (Holocene status) has become *Homo deus* (Anthropocene reality), does the iron rule of empires (they fall) hold for Earth as human empire? The reality is that modernity's dream—exercising mastery over unruly nature—failed. Instead we've bound ourselves fatefully to Earth as a single, wild evolving force. There is no "outside" for us or Archimedean point. There never was. There was only more room for error and weaker powers. Nature has always included us.

It's rather ironic, isn't it, that just when we realize we're major players in a no-analog world, we discover we're a lot less important than we thought. Wild Earth can get along fine without us. For most of its life, it has.

Whether Earth as human empire will fail on a grand scale, I can't possibly say. Leave that to students of "collapsology." Clearly, however, climate stability as the matrix for human empire is history. The Holocene's over. Our Anthropocene powers yield less control than we assumed and create more chaos.

So how do we exercise responsibility? Certainly not by looking away. When we look away or substitute wishful thinking for hope, the world grows more perilous. To repeat Coffin, the world is too dangerous for anything but truth and too small for anything but love. The best leaders forge ahead amid dangers they face honestly.

Still, the perilous future is not the place to *begin* an account of responsibility. That's Frankl's *Yes to Life: In Spite of Everything.*

For Frankl, at work again as a psychotherapist after his liberation from the death camps, it doesn't matter whether we live in the Holocene or Anthropocene. There is something so elemental about being responsible that it crosses all times and places. It's primordial: "The great fundamental truth of being human is nothing other than being conscious and being responsible!"

Being conscious is simply being alive. And being both alive and responsible is the truth of being human. For Frankl, that truth is in play until our very last breath as individuals and our last breath as a species. What we are responsible for, anytime, anywhere, under any conditions, is the meaning of life. He saw camp inmates exercising a freedom no one could take from them— granting meaning to their life even as it ended, dying on their own inner terms even as someone else was ending their life in every other way. Response-ability was theirs to the end and in the end. They didn't abdicate.

What responsibility means in the Anthropocene will be clearer if we see how the changing planet has changed it.

The roots of this change are in the Holocene. Upending natural world norms came about with a fossil-fueled way of life that over two centuries, and especially after 1950, reset Earth's thermostat and altered the climate system itself. Care was not given to what earth (soil), air, fire (energy), and water required for their own renewal on their own terms. *Sapiens* could dominate the rest of nature on human terms and, to a remarkable degree, has.

Still, the agents were not human beings acting as a single tribe. The agents were those who fashioned the modern world on the basis of slavery, colonization, conquest, and consumerism through a profit-driven mode of living. They dominated both nature and peoples together. This not only happened in the Holocene; it ended the Holocene.

What's patently unfair is that you, as Anthropocene kids, did not create the problems you're inheriting, but you're going to be responsible for them to some degree throughout your lives. The question now is not whether you will have to confront climate change but how you will respond, as individuals and collectively.

While all humans and the full community of life suffer the consequences of climate system change, and all will be forced to respond in some manner or another, not all are responsible in the same way to the same degree. All in the same storm doesn't mean all in the same boat.

Some owe more than others because their carbon footprint is far greater, as are their powers. Justice requires *common but differentiated responsibilities and relative capacities* (the language of the UN and the IPCC).

I'll come back to that. But I want to start with an unforgiving element of Anthropocene responsibility, as clear as desert air after a rain: Greenhouse gases must not exceed the planet's "sinks" for them. That boundary cannot be moved. It's hard, fast, and brittle. We must stay at or below Earth's sequestrations of greenhouse gases. No more important measure of responsibility exists than holding the sequestration line, for survival's sake.

How is your responsibility different from Grandma Nyla's and mine? I can tell you why our notion and practice of responsibility failed, however well-meant.

From the Industrial Revolution onward, most people, some Indigenous peoples excepted, conceived responsibility as human to human. A responsible person was one who shared human burdens and benefits fairly in the interest of furthering human well-being. Reigning moral norms—love and justice—gave noble voice to this. But these norms were intra-human only.

Our sense of responsibility also assumed that the basic unit of human survival is human society. It is not. The planet you inherit is. But we left ecospheric essentials sitting outside assumed human responsibility. We rendered nonhuman elements and other-than-human lives as something tangential to our moral framework. We wrongly believed that "nonhuman" was beyond our responsibility.

All of this means that you will need to reform responsibility in keeping with Thomas Berry: "Planetary well-being is primary; human well-being is derivative." That means there are differentiated responsibilities *between* humans and the rest of life as well as differentiated responsibilities *within* the human family. The primal elements of earth, air, fire, and water, and their claims for their health on their own terms, belong to Anthropocene responsibility.

What are your future choices? Scientists Simon Lewis and Mark Maslin outline three. Continue developing our consumer capitalist mode of living is one. This is the (very) late Holocene default as millions process behind the crucifix of Capitalist Progress. Suffering widespread civilizational collapse is a second possible future. Making our dogged way to a new mode of living is the third.

Earth can't afford more black belts in buying and using up. So as best I can judge, if Lewis and Maslin's first option is realized, it leads to the second—collapse. The forced option, then, is the third, an altered way of life. It's forced because it cannot be avoided. Yet it's truly an option because it must be consciously chosen.

That new mode of living is the subject of our final letters. Meanwhile, I'd like to think about how we think about responsibility. Remember, *how* we think about things determines *what* we think and subsequently *do*.

The statement of changed conditions was offered nearly forty years ago, before we even had a conceptual framework for those changes. (Neither "Holocene" nor "Anthropocene" shaped anyone's thinking then.)

Hans Jonas published *The Imperative of Responsibility* in 1984. "The altered nature of human action," he wrote, "and the lengthened reach of our deeds moves *responsibility*, with no less than man's fate for its object, into the centre of the ethical stage." Complicating efforts to adapt responsibility to the "altered nature of human action" is this: Our powers and their technological means gave birth to consequences so far-reaching in time and space that we can't begin to know all we do. And when we don't know, we can't take responsibility. How do we love human and other-than-human neighbors whom we can't see, don't see, and won't see? Their living conditions and needs are out of sight, yet their fate rides on our actions. How do we hold ourselves accountable for such far-flung consequences? What sense can responsibility make if it falls short of the actual outcome of our powers?

Yet we can know what brought on the Anthropocene and what can and should be done in keeping with common but differentiated responsibilities. Chief among these is dismantling white-created and dominated institutions as those play out in the high-carbon lifestyle they bring. Systemic inequality, racism, gender oppression, and domination of nature's systems have all served the wealthy and privileged. Utah Phillips is right: "Earth is not dying; it is being killed. And the people who are killing it have names and addresses." Those are the names and addresses of the wealthiest 10 percent of Earth's population. They produce half of all carbon emissions, while the poorest half of the population is responsible for only 10 percent of emissions. It's a bitter injustice that those who contribute least to natural world change suffer the most, while those who contribute most suffer the least. The well-off buffer themselves, but not the rest, from the worst consequences of their own way of life.

In short, we know we must put an end to a growing, extractive economy running on ecological deficits, together with an end to wealth that trickles up rather than down. The "heedlessness of [this kind of] global marketplace" led to the late Holocene's "depredation, depletion, and disruptive climate change." It's our job to overcome these Holocene habits and ask what the Anthropocene requires. That's nothing less than a different relationship of *sapiens* to Earth. From that relationship might radiate responsibility adapted to altered conditions. That's where we're going.

Daunting as it is, I'm excited about it! Hope you are too. I think of you both all the time.

Abrazos!

Grandpa

IT'S ALL IN THE PRONOUNS

October 25, 2020

Dear Eduardo and Martín,

We're discussing responsibility. I know you two argue about that. Thomas the Train Engine is missing; where is he? Who knocked down the Lego towers? Who's responsible?

Our discussion is different. We're asking how we think imaginatively about swelling human powers. Specifically, we're looking for a human-Earth relationship that radiates responsibility amid profoundly altered planetary conditions.

I wrote earlier about *Braiding Sweetgrass.* The author, Robin Wall Kimmerer, captures our changed circumstances and overall responsibility better than anyone: "From the beginning of the world, the other species were a lifeboat for the people. Now, we must be theirs." That is Anthropocene responsibility.

What would it mean to be the lifeboat for other species as well as ourselves, to be Noah's Ark as Earth's Ark? Two wee sentences may be all we need: "It's all in the pronouns" and "All flourishing is mutual."

"It's all in the pronouns." Our laptop screensaver is you, Eduardo, in your chef's hat and chef's apron, standing on a stool to work with Grandma Nyla on the cake for your third birthday. You were, at the time, a close friend to every kind of truck. Well, Grandma Nyla found instructions for a multicolored, multitiered dump-truck birthday cake that you and she spent hours making. It was spectacular! I think the only part you two didn't manage from scratch were the wheels. You fudged and bought chocolate-covered donuts.

As Grandma made the truck, you didn't say to your mom, "It's making the cab now." Grandma was never an "it." You and "it" didn't make the cake. Grandma was a "she" and a person. Even your three-year-old vocabulary knew that she, like you, was another subject, not an object. Your relationship was lodged in the pronouns.

Cultures, not just individual persons, are shaped by pronoun relationships. Let's call them "we-it" and "we-thou" relationships—subject-object and subject-subject. "I-thou" and "we-thou" relationships, as subject to subject, are connections of attachment and intimacy. In contrast, "I-it" and "we-it" relationships, as subject to object, are marked by detachment and distance. Thinking of something as an "it" automatically separates and objectifies. It's a one-way relationship, if it can even be called a relationship when there's no back and forth.

Kimmerer is a botanist who both studies plants subject to object and learns from them subject to subject. They respond to her and she to them (she knows their languages). There is flourishing, and the flourishing is mutual. It's personal too. The plant world isn't a big "it" to her. The citizens are "persons." She speaks of the maple and pecan nations and the bird and plant families.

How we picture the Earth-human connection is radically different. Consider the dominant relationship that Holocene industrial economies have had with Earth: it's we-it all the way. Human subjects prize objects for their utility, period. Nature is not evidence piled atop evidence that Earth is profoundly alive, living the grammar of animacy, like it is for Kimmerer and Indigenous peoples. Rather, most Holoceners have viewed nature as a vast collection of malleable objects. "Natural capital" and "natural resources" serve human purposes, as all capital and resources do. And the relationship is unidirectional and detached. We take without giving. Or if we do give, it's only in order to do more taking. We keep taking until Earth rebels.

For a long stretch, Rex Tillerson was the CEO of Exxon-Mobil. Every year running, a small number of shareholders filed an annual petition that the oil and gas company stop using the atmosphere as, in effect, a sewer. They argued that polluting the atmosphere was wrong even if it provided invaluable energy. In one shareholder discussion, an apparently exasperated Tillerson replied with a question that was meant to settle the matter: "What good is it to save the planet if humanity suffers?" No "good" at all, in his limited view.

Tillerson's doctrine of creation had its counterpart in the question of Jason Bostic of the West Virginia Coal Association: "What good is a mountain just to have a mountain?" he asked. For Tillerson and Bostic, the value of the planet and the mountain—their "good"—is their use value for an anthropocentric world. They are only "good" insofar as humans can extract resources from them.

Often, I-it and we-it dominate human relationships too. The father of Black theology, James Cone, gave an address in 1998 at Union in which he argued that "the logic that led to slavery and segregation in the Americas, colonization and apartheid in Africa, and the rule of white supremacy throughout the world is the same one that leads to the exploitation of animals and the ravaging of nature." He noted that the "mechanistic and instrumental logic" of exploitation "defines everything and everybody in terms of their contribution to the development and defense of white world supremacy."

Remember this: "It's all in the pronouns." If people, animals, and the rest of nature are "it" alone, the logic of use is instrumental and mechanistic. "Its" value is its usefulness to humans, at least some humans (the white world, in Cone's argument). This is the heart of consumerism. Consumerism is a use-centered way of life for meeting human needs and desires and nothing more. And this will continue as the commonsense relationship unless you in the Anthropocene find a way to reimagine responsibility itself.

You can take Kimmerer as a model here. Her pronouns of first choice are different, as is their logic. Kimmerer, who is Potawatomi, uses language akin to that of the Aboriginal Indigenous Peoples' Council in "Beyond Climate Change to Survival on Sacred Mother Earth," a statement to the United Nations in 2014. The first paragraph reads: "All Creation has a right to live and survive on this Sacred Earth and raise their Families where the Creator placed them to be." A later paragraph says, "To survive climate change and see the future we must restore the sacred in ourselves and include the sacredness of all life in our discussions, decisions, and actions."

The logic of I-it and we-it knows nothing of the "sacredness of all life" or of creation's "families" as other than human families. It doesn't recognize the forest people (trees) or the plant people, the Maple nation or the bird nations, and treat them morally as persons. The relationship is not personal at all, not *this always attached to that* for better and worse until death us do part.

Here *sacred* means the inherent value attached to citizens of a subject-subject world rather than the planet as the subject-object world that awaits human value for whatever meaning we give it.

Sacred is also Kimmerer's webbed world in which "there are no soloists." "All flourishing is mutual," she says. This magnifies the presence and meaning of the interacting elements. Surviving and thriving require a "covenant of reciprocity, a pact of mutual responsibility to sustain those who sustain us." Earth's Ark as Noah's Ark.

While we take care of plants, plants also take care of us. What they breathe out, we breathe in. If they stop breathing, so do we. We take care of animals, to be sure, but for millennia we haven't been able to live without them, either—for work, food, and companionship. We take care of the air, water, and soil, while they have also taken care of us in the most elemental ways, from the day we arrived and for as long as we have taken breath and fixed breakfast. They have, for our sake, been instrumental for our life; now we must give back and be instrumental for theirs. When both their well-being and ours are in jeopardy, we must reciprocate and be their lifeboat as well.

But do our biotic and abiotic neighbors exercise responsibility? If they do, that likely changes our understanding of responsibility itself.

Recall that all life responds to that which acts upon it. It is "response-able" and "respons-ive." Remember also what Frankl said, that responsibility is co-terminus with life itself. This responsibility may not be the same edition of responsibility as human agency provides. Nor would rights attached to other-than-human responsibility be the same version as human rights. It's silly to say that only human rights are important. That, for example, if other life can't freely assemble, exercise free speech, bear arms, and vote, it doesn't have rights. There can be different editions of rights for different entities—for mountains and rivers, for animals, even for those essential microorganisms. For Kimmerer and the Indigenous Peoples' Council, lacking strict *sapien* analogs doesn't mean that other-than-*sapien* life lacks duties and responsibilities. Kimmerer speaks of how water is faithful "to its responsibility, every day."

Pursuing this, she cites *The Thanksgiving Address: Greetings to the Natural World*. Also called *The Words Before All Else*, the *Address* is likely a thousand years old and is used as a guiding principle of Haudenosaunee culture. Its theme is gratitude, and it proceeds with a roll call that greets all creatures and gives thanks for them, together with thanks for the primal elements and abiotic "persons" like the sun, moon, winds, and rain. Each of the natural "persons" is greeted and given thanks—"The Earth Mother, The Waters, The Fish, The Plants, The Food Plants, The Medicine Herbs, The Animals, The Trees, The Birds, The Four Winds, The Thunderers, The Sun, Grandmother Moon, The Stars, The Enlightened Teachers, and The Creator."

I'm struck by the way the Haudenosaunee are communing here with all the elements of life. Greetings are extended and thanks are offered as the way to begin the day and center the mind. Intelligences other than our own are present. Give heed.

The address makes clear that all the persons of the natural world have their duties, as do humans. Kimmerer cites but one, the Waters, who are thanked for "doing their duty of sustaining life on Mother Earth. Water is life, quenching our thirst and sustaining us all. Let us gather our minds together and, with one mind, we send greetings and thanks to the Waters."

Waters have responsibility for sustaining life. But to carry out their duties and do what they do requires that we depart from the we-it detachment of industrial and postindustrial culture and recognize waters' claims upon us for their well-being. They make moral claims on us. The right relationship is reciprocal. If we do not do our part, they cannot do theirs. Flourishing is mutual.

The sun's setting; it's suppertime and soon your bedtime. Like the Thanksgiving Address, I send you greetings and give thanks for each of you and both of you. I have not intended to leave anything out, but if I have, I leave it to each of you to send greetings and thanks to all life in your own wonderful childlike way.

But before bed, we should see what has come of our meditation on who we are and what the nature of human nature means for Anthropocene responsibility. Try this.

In the Anthropocene, our deep, far-reaching interconnectedness will be dramatically, sometimes frightfully, apparent. You'll find that we're all too human in the best and worst ways, as we were in the Holocene. You can count on community impulse and tribalism, simplifying and othering, as common practice, for better and worse. You can also count on bursts of astounding collective creativity amid changed and changing planetary conditions. Cultural diversity may well form and transform human action in the Anthropocene in ways Grandma Nyla and I never knew. That diversity amid crises will probably not transform human nature, however, except over millennia. Evolution and stones tell time and stories differently than we do. We'll not see the big changes in brains that might slowly happen. We might, however, create altered genomes for rapid changes we hardly dared imagine.

The open-endedness of symbolic and reflective consciousness may be your best asset, even though it won't likely alter our nature as twinned good and evil. Any pod of children you see at birth could grow up to be Winston Churchill, the Dalai Lama, Donald Trump, Idi Amin, Dorothy Day, Ruth Bader Ginsburg, Muhammad Ali, or LeBron James. The Anthropocene won't delete sin, goodness, wonder, variety, or surprise.

Since power is the tattoo of your epoch, attend to it always, as energy and capacity and as love, influence, and coercion. Niebuhr and King offer their wisdom for your organizing and governing aspirations even if their notions are too Holocene, meaning intra-human only.

I'm keenly aware that we've touched upon only some of your Anthropocene powers and maybe not the most far-reaching ones. We've only mentioned the pretty much endless powers of genetic manipulation "to rewrite the very molecules of life any way we wish." We've said even less about artificial intelligence and robotics. While I can't begin to fathom what these might mean for planetary life and death in human hands, I'm certain they mandate attention to how these powers are exercised in a world they see, and treat, as drastically subject-to-object.

Even with such manipulative powers, *especially* with such powers, I hope you see it as your responsibility to be in relationship with the whole community of life. Watch your language, especially pronouns! Treat everything "personally" and with reciprocity, as though microcosm and macrocosm are as real as the universe thinks they are. Extend the sense of sacredness that the soul knows to all things great and small.

I know this doesn't answer the conundrums we raised in the previous letter about matching responsibility to the time and space consequences of our actions. That's a book in itself, maybe yours. I make only two proposals. First, start with your own household and community rather than global supply lines. See what can be done with the people and resources you have, treated "personally" across the community of life in your locale. Branch out from there as circumstances require (climate calamity and pandemics necessitate global cooperation attached to local efforts).

Second, look to the kind of relationship human responsibility can best count on for the good of all for the long haul, even when we cannot see distant outcomes. That's nonviolent love. Sometimes it appears in kind, soft forms, but at other times, it's coercive prophetic power for systemic transformation. How might Anthropocene powers be wielded nonviolently?

Optimally, justice-love relationships include enemies. We noted earlier that we're all in the same storm and in the same *polder* now. That means loving the neighbor or else, whoever the neighbor is. It also means avoiding we-they tribalisms that work from stereotypes rather than acknowledged complexity. Too, look for the creative act amid conflict, one that thinks outside the box in order to build new boxes. Nonviolent love seems the most promising path in a world too small and dangerous for anything but truth and love.

All of this will, I pray, serve your generation's vocation as the first citizens of the Anthropocene undertaking a new Great Work.

Martín Theo, God won't be departing anytime soon, either. So hang on to your name. Meditate with Eduardo on Living Presence as the hovering love that moves "the sun and other stars," as Dante said. We send you both a dusting.

We love you so much,

Grandpa and Grandma

BECOMING GOOD ANCESTORS

Dear Eduardo, dear Martín,

You're six today, Eduardo! But your dad says you tested positive for COVID-19. We're very relieved you rebounded quickly, but we certainly understand your question, "Why does a kid get COVID on his birthday?" Not fair!

Grandma Nyla and I wish we were there. We'll come as soon as King Corona lowers the drawbridge.

While COVID-19 is our immediate concern, the bigger picture is the future you and Martín might incubate and the good ancestors you might become. When you read this, you'll be engaging your Great Work and answering the old preacher's question, "What are you going to do with the dash in your life, the dash on your tombstone between your birth date and death date?" It's Mary Oliver's question as well: "Tell me, what is it you plan to do with your one wild and precious life?"

Grandpa love makes me want to think together about what goes into any Anthropocene way of life. We can sketch the essential elements even if we can't dictate the details.

For those essentials, we'll build cairns. Cairns are small stone towers that serve as points of reference where the trail doesn't yet exist or is easily lost.

Cairns aren't the path itself—you make the path by walking it. But cairns let you see where you are and where the next leg might be.

You'll traverse unknown territory. This is *aftertime* work where you both build cairns and create the path. You'll draw upon the past—those other Great Works—and be inspired that the impossible has been done before. I'll name cairns to mark your way as your generation strives to do the impossible again. These cairns are not separate. Change in one evokes change elsewhere. They interact as a way-of-life ecosystem.

There are several things to say as you make your way. The first is a reminder that the Anthropocene is our doing. Never before have human choices and actions effected a new geological epoch. While planetary systems have always had a heavy hand in plotting the play and directing the human drama, never have all the planetary spheres been so profoundly altered by *sapien* powers. Previous powers did not revamp the chemistry of the atmosphere, the hydrosphere, and the cryosphere (water and ice); wrinkle the lithosphere (the Earth's crust); or bludgeon the biosphere (the community of life). As an evolutionary force, we are remaking the planet in ways that merge geological time with human time and that smudge the line between moral evil and natural disasters (we're both ark and flood). This means that in the Anthropocene everything, including extinction, turns on ethics (our choices and actions).

The second thing to say is this. The Stone Age didn't end because we ran out of stones, and our present age won't end because we ran out of fossil fuels. The Stone Age ended because the Bronze Age began, and the fossil fuel age will end when all the vital work can be done by sun, wind, tides, geothermal energy, hydrogen, maybe nuclear fusion, and other renewables. Nonetheless, oil, gas, and coal will still be around to fight for Lewis and Maslin's first option—the urge to continue, even expand, our consumer capitalist lifeway. You should therefore expect plenty of battles around the elements that follow. My discussion doesn't dwell on the battles, however, but on the elements themselves—cosmology, community, ethics, ritual, and inner journey. These are Great Work cairns.

They aren't the only cairns, however. There are four at the trailhead: Love. Mourn. Organize. Heal. Sit with those for a while. You can't take them with you. Cairns aren't meant to be transported, and you don't want stones in your backpacks, in any case. But these cairns are markers of Anthropocene responsibility, so internalize them and come back to them now and again as matters of mind and heart.

Here are the cairns on the trail.

Cosmology. Our first cairn is cosmology, which is a way of beholding everything around us. It's how we absorb reality and interpret it. It's the container for our basic perspective on the world and on life.

Most of this beholding happens subconsciously. So if you ask your neighbor, "How's your cosmology today, Charlie? Serving you well? Just checking," you'll get a stare rather than an answer.

I don't mean scientific cosmology—that's how the material universe began and is structured. I mean philosophical, religious, and cultural cosmology. They take in and make sense of what we experience. Some call it *worldview* or *gaze*.

Cosmologies work like compasses and gyroscopes. They set our direction and keep us upright so that our day-to-day bearing doesn't fly to pieces.

The question for you is how the Anthropocene might shape your cosmology. It's clear the planet will be less hospitable for you than it was for us. Still, Grandma Nyla and I live as though the institutions and systems that formed us will continue. We make breakfast, lunch, and dinner the same way. Which is to say that our cosmology hasn't caught up with reality, so our way of life hasn't either. Old ways hang on us like comfy clothes even as an emerging epoch grows more violent.

It's easy to fall into paralysis when I learn how deep and long-lasting the effects of Anthropocene powers are. Consider this. Paleo-climatologists studying planetary cycles tell us that Holoceners were due to move into the next ice age in fifty thousand years. But our global warming, most of it since 1950, has suppressed that ice age cycle and perhaps the one due in 130 thousand years. Without the foggiest notion of what we're doing, we've overridden some of the planet's most ingrained patterns. That holds for immediate patterns—this year's fire season, next year's weather—as well as those so far out of sight we can't take them in, like ice age returns.

What do I do when the morality I most rely upon is obsolete, namely making decisions and choosing actions by weighing their consequences? How can we be accountable to future generations when our powers put them out of sight? Who even fathoms that we are creating deep futures? Yet we are collectively deciding—if "deciding" is the right word—about sea-level rise, energy, land use, and dying forests.

Fortunately, numerous organizations consciously moving to take responsibility are explicit about their cosmology as they do so. I'll cite but one even though the internet blooms with new initiatives daily. That's a hopeful sign. We're serious about saving ourselves.

GreenFaith is an interfaith, international organization helping to effect planetary healing through advocacy work and a variety of training programs. Its vision statement captures the way its members behold the world. "We envision a world transformed, in which humanity in all its diversity has developed a shared reverence for life on Earth," it says. It references "the sacredness of Earth and the dignity of all people" and notes that "the era of conquest, extraction, and exploitation has given way to cooperation and community."

I can't know what your cosmology should be. I do urge one that begins with creation as sacred—GreenFaith's "shared reverence for life on Earth." Earth as a sacred trust is the place to start: seeing the ordinary in an extraordinary light. It's Marilynne Robinson's daily ordinary as "dear," it's Kimmerer's world as "magnified," and it's second-century Irenaeus's vision of a world in which "the glory of God is humanity fully alive." It's forests as sacred groves, not just timber, and other species as kin, not just resources.

Community. Whether on the grandest scale or the most minute, creation is internally related. A deep "togetherness" holds; nothing is itself apart from all else. Our second cairn of community, whatever its many forms, is derived from this primordial communion. To be good ancestors means creating sustainable communities in healthy bioregions where responsibility entails mutual flourishing.

Let's be clear: Community responsibility in the Anthropocene is different from the Holocene's. For the Anthropocene, responsibility is reciprocal in a gathering of subjects across the whole community of life. For many modern humans, the depth and breadth of this interaction is new responsibility. For some—most Indigenous communities—it's renewed.

Now couple reciprocal responsibility to what we've highlighted about human repair, namely addressing systemic inequality and race disparities and securing social justice as essential to creation justice.

Ethics. We've pointed to ethics, our third cairn, multiple times already. My main point was that many long-held Holocene moral norms and habits no longer suffice. So what *will* suffice? How will Anthropocene ethics proceed as you move from human industrial civilization to ecological civilization?

However it proceeds, it will attend to what ethics is at heart. That's the moral formation of persons and their institutions, as well as the moral *trans*formation of both when repair is needed.

One way to map out a better future is to retrieve an ancient vision that both forms and reforms in the manner not only of ethics but cosmology and community too—*oikos.* (Here go the Greeks again!)

Oikos, Greek for "house" and "household," is the root of "economy," "ecology," and "ecumenics." All our "eco" words stem from a vision of shared life in the same household—Habitat Earth, in this case. *Economics* means knowing how things work and managing "home systems" (ecosystems) in such a way that the material requirements of the household of life are met and sustained. *Economics* literally means "the house rules."

In this vision, Earth is a vast but single household of life. It's the *oikoumenē*, the "whole inhabited Earth." The upbuilding of this household is community formation and sustenance, which requires intimate knowledge of how the community works. That's what *ecology* means—knowing how things work in relation to one another and sustaining that for the well-being of all. (*Ecology* is *oikos* + *logos*, the "logic" of the household.)

Of course, *oikos* isn't truly the common household for human and other-than-human life unless justice reigns, unless the whole planet receives its due. Short of that, *oikos* may be home to some while others are rendered, well, homeless.

These "eco" words and their vision map the interacting requirements for life's continuation in the Anthropocene. If the *oikos* example seems far-fetched to you, it's far-fetched for a reason. The reason is that post-Industrial Revolution economies, the only kind you've known, separated economy from environment, commerce from creation care, and human neighbors from other-than-human. Modern human economies abandoned the household and its community as the center of economic life and replaced them with the firm or corporation.

The long-term interests of corporations and firms are very different from those of households and communities. Market share and maximum profits are the preoccupation of corporations and firms. But they aren't the driving force of households. Quality of life is. How might economy, ecology, and ecumenics together foster household quality of life? That's the *oikos* quest and the work of ethics.

Ritual. "Rituals are the core of every community's life," write theologians Rita Nakashima Brock and Rebecca Parker. That won't be different for you. They are "like the bones of a body's skeleton, the framework that holds things into a shape, giving form to a community's values and relationships." They're the containers for the peak moments that touch every life and every community. And they're remembered in forms more powerful than words alone.

We ritualize everything: eating, meeting strangers, resolving conflicts, mating, and rites of passage like births, birthdays, and deaths. The question for you is not whether ritual and "ceremony" (the Indigenous term) are critical for the meaning you find or create. The question is which rituals and ceremonies are vital for your epoch.

Some might be old—tested and true. Others might be wholly new, sparked by the creativity a unique epoch requires. (Should you hold funerals for dying coral reefs or forests? What about celebrations for implanted genes that prevent inherited deadly diseases and deformities?) Whether old, new, or hybridized, rituals embody meaning in highly accessible, dramatic ways. It's no surprise that life both begins with ritual (naming and dedicating a baby) and ends with it (treating the deceased and caring for their loved ones).

Let's do a roll call of rituals we've noted. Recall Berlin in the days after President Kennedy was assassinated. Candles in the darkened windows of East Berlin were impromptu rituals that captured the mourning and respect of thousands. They paid tribute in the simplest way—candlelight defeating darkness.

And a few weeks ago, in Washington, DC, the Reflecting Pool was lined with four hundred lanterns stretching from the Lincoln Memorial to the Washington Monument, each lantern symbolizing one thousand COVID-19 deaths. It was silent and beautiful, as heavy with sorrow as the humid night air itself.

In the Anthropocene, it will be important to mark the grief of losses we've inflicted on the planet. That's why Mourn is a trailhead cairn.

Some of this is already underway. "Prayers in the Ashes" was an Ash Wednesday service in the cinders of the Thomas Fire near Ojai, California. Though Ash Wednesday is a Christian observance, this was interfaith collaboration with Chumash (Indigenous), Shinto, and Christian leadership. It was hosted by Ojai's Church of the Wild, an outdoor-worshipping community.

Participants, standing in a circle amid the forest ashes, shared a lament. Each petition ended with "the land is devastated" and the response, "We have no words." Participants grieved the flames that "devour canyons and meadow, riverbeds and mountains" and the damage done to "live oak, Manzanita, monkeyflower, and sage; olive, willow, lilacs, and lupine." The litany ends, "When what we love is ashes, the winds bring little rain, our taxes fuel insanity, that land and our hearts are devastated." Participants respond, "We have no words." A long silence follows and then "And into this no-words we listen." Thereafter, time is given for meditation as participants wander to different places in the ashes. When regathered, there is a Shinto cleansing rite, and ashes from the forest floor are pressed to participants' foreheads as they voice compassion for this place as holy ground.

Participants from various traditions worked out the ritual together and then crafted it to include the wild creatures of the land and its waters, the scorched rocks and charred remains of the forest and its life, and humans.

I note another ritual, one at Union Seminary. The James Chapel floor hosted a mound of soil. Worshippers brought plants to the mound, sat next to them, and publicly confessed their sins against the natural world. "I never said 'thanks' to the tree of my childhood where I spent endless hours," said one. Another was inwardly unprepared: "I don't know how to relate to you in this subjective way," she said to the plants. "I am afraid that if I do I might discover a level of pain that I don't know whether I can bear." That service, only glimpsed here, went viral, with internet responses ranging from tears of gratitude to condemnation as paganism.

Your experience may be that rituals like these elicit provocation. They do so because they operate in a different register. What happened in the Union ritual and the Thomas fire gathering was that the barrier between subjectivity and objectivity fell away completely. All present became interactive subjects. Everything was personal. Rituals create this interlaced subjectivity. They form people, communities, and cosmologies.

Inner Journey. "Happiness is an inside job" is an old adage. But happiness is not only an inside job; it's an outside one, too, because every way of life is both internalized and publicly embodied.

Inner and outer journeys are invariably connected, with some kind of spirituality present. There's some cluster of feelings, some story, some values, some culture or subculture, and some hunger for connection.

To see inner and outer journeys always connected, imagine what your mind, imagination, and spirituality would be if all you knew were a barren lunar landscape. No birds, no forests, no mountains or plains, no artistic or musical renderings of these, no other human beings or other animals, no stories, no bowls of fruit, no bread or desserts, no chocolate or licorice, no . . . well, you get the picture. If all that meets your eye is an utterly barren moonscape, and it's all your memory knows, your imagination will be equally barren, with no images to stoke it. What would inhabit your inner journey if there were no flowing streams, buzzing insects, musicians, or V-lines of geese gliding in the air? In no time, we would realize that all reality, including Living Presence, communicates through nature. Though I know it's not possible, try erasing all images of Earth, including those stored in your memory. You would have no spirit at all. Maybe no mind, either.

What this exercise demonstrates is that outer and inner feed one another. The mind-boggling dimensions of Anthropocene responsibility, with its obligation toward the whole of earthly life, require attending to this kind of spiritual and moral formation. Of course, you'll need the best technology and engineering you can muster, the best science and analysis. But of themselves they do not achieve a spiritually rich way of life. Nor do science and technology cultivate tender feelings for the sacred and a keen awareness of it. Reverence for Earth requires loving attention and spirited attachment. What is not loved is lost.

None of this escapes the inner journey as a place of conflict where spirits battle one another. Because no human platform has ever guaranteed happiness or known virtue immune from vice, there will always be spiritual struggle. You may be familiar with the Cherokee grandpa-and-grandson tale about the two wolves inside every person. One wolf is angry, greedy, and unhappy, spreading lies and stoking divisions; the other is beautiful and good, practicing kindness, generosity, and compassion. These two wolves are always fighting with one another, the grandfather explains.

"Oyee!" cries the boy. "Grandfather, which wolf will win this horrific war?"

The grandfather replies, "The wolf that you feed. That wolf will surely win!"

Here, then, are your cairns. Love. Mourn. Organize. Heal at the trailhead. Then, as you undertake your Great Work, these five, all tuned to the Anthropocene.

Cosmology beholds the world and sets your basic orientation. In the Anthropocene, what is best would be to view the entire natural realm, ourselves included, as sacred.

Community for you is the expanded world, internally related so as to carry human responsibility for planetary well-being.

Ethics is about creating cultural values, norms, and institutions that encourage the mutual flourishing of both human and other-than-human worlds.

Ritual will let you share the distilled meaning of your new era—collectively acknowledging wrongdoing, grieving losses, and celebrating new life wherever it emerges.

The inner journey points to the vital role of cultivating spirituality for life in a new epoch.

These are the ecosystemic elements present in whatever mode of living you incubate for Anthropocene life.

I have parting words and a final letter, so I'll close here. You know how much I love you.

Abrazos!

Grandpa

LEAVING A LEGACY

April 4, 2021

Dear Eduardo, dear Martín,

These are love letters from first to last. In the very first one, love bridges geological epochs. Spud hadn't yet made his grand entrance, so that letter's only to you, Eduardo. (But you told us he was on his way, "swimming in Mommy's tummy.")

This one, to both of you, will end the same—with love bridging from our world to yours. Despite that love, or because of it, writing has been wrenching at times. Why should you be saddled with a *global civilizational challenge* amid a *geological shift* in a *no-analog world*?

Unexpected crises made the letters difficult, and deep enough that the planet's physical tumult and social chaos began to feel like the loss of worlds African and Indigenous peoples have long experienced. Somehow, they had to survive loss of their civilizations and land, only to begin again on alien terrain. While *the* world did not end, some worlds did. Their worlds did. Now that's reality for even more than the colonized.

The outcome is a stack of uncharted challenges and the need for a different Great Work. If there's a humorous version, it's Pogo's: "What we face, friends, are insurmountable opportunities." Insurmountable opportunities. What's the rigging for those?

It includes radical honesty. The early Anthropocene is already baked in to such an extent that your world simply will not escape immense suffering together with displaced peoples, flora, and fauna. Nor will compromise and defeat be avoided. Wild cards guarantee uncertainty as the one sure thing. Big, complex, interacting systems, determining futures you cannot control, will ratchet up risk, frustrate the best of intentions, and assure failures. Life dishes up more than we can plan for, some of which will turn out to be wonderfully good, but much will not. In any case, all of it mandates radical realism. Baldwin is right again: "Not everything that is faced can be changed, but nothing can be changed until it is faced."

This takes a toll. And the toll is greater, not less, when remaking the world is your calling and you love what you're doing. That's love's cruel side: pain, loss, and responsibility are more poignant when you care.

Don't push away the pain. Accept it. It's not there by accident; it's a life imperative. On the other side is healing and new resolve.

President Barack and Michelle Obama were in Oslo in 2009 to receive the Nobel Peace Prize. The president was coming off a very difficult time in the White House, agonizing over ongoing wars in Iraq and Afghanistan. He would return to that and much more, not least an impasse on healthcare legislation and the Great Recession. As the Obamas were about to leave their hotel for the Nobel dinner, one of the American delegation knocked on the door and told them to look out the window. They opened the drapes, and there were several thousand people, each holding a candle—the traditional ritual for the city to salute the Peace Prize recipient. When the Obamas appeared, the crowd cheered wildly. Here, amid the president's preoccupation with agonies that wouldn't pause, was "a pool of stars" held aloft by those who refused to give up on the idea that the world could be better. President Obama's response to himself was, *"Whatever you do won't be enough,* I heard their voices say. *Try anyway."*

Obama did not achieve everything he wanted to. Oddly, failure while trying anyway is a fine criterion. If what you want to do with your tombstone dash isn't big enough to risk failure and multiple tries, some of which will fail, then your vision and goal are too humble, too shallow, too unworthy of your one precious life.

So accept the wisdom that, because remapping and remaking is civilizational work in a no-analog world, "whatever you do will not be enough." It cannot be. If nothing else, your lives, however long, will not be long enough. You belong to a vital transitional generation, but that's not the generation that slaps the final coat of paint on the wall or gets to spit-polish shoes for the victory dance.

Do you recall my response to Niebuhr and Baldwin about race reckoning, that it still needed a century? My generation's idealism was dashed by that prospect. But the two of them waded in with renewed energy. To them a century of good work for undoing legacies as deep as race and caste seemed hopeful and realistic. So take your first steps and make your way knowing others will add more cairns. The stones will keep talking.

Still, my generation's impatience was right in one way. It's vital to dream an ideal world and go big, with confidence.

Especially the young often get things done because they didn't know they couldn't. "Impossible" gets nudged into the "possible" column.

So dream a world and lace it with a little utopia. That's a world that levels the standard of living, with a steady-state economy attentive to Earth's regeneration. A world of jobs and healthcare for all in need of them. A world where quality of life for household and community is the economy's purpose and focus, not the profits of big firms and corporations. A world of widespread public transportation in and between green cities. A world of clean renewable energy sources. A world of diets low in the use of animals. A world where spiritual well-being replaces gaudy consumerism. A world where diversity plays out as strength, not inequity, and where colonialist and environmental debt is settled with reparations on the way to liberty and justice for all. A world attentive to the *whole* community of life and its glory, with *sapiens* present neither as "devils nor divines" but the world's "true wonder." And not least, a world full of music: while music can't cure everything, with it you can sing down the grimness in front of you.

Add your dreams to these, with Dr. King's Beloved Community in view and Amanda Gorman in your ears: "[O]ne thing is certain. If we merge mercy with might, and might with right, then love becomes our legacy and change our children's birthright."

Yours is certainly not a moment for caution. Toss it! And resist the advice of those who say, "Never try anything the first time around!"

It's fine to start small and to get help. In the raised bed on your deck, I've seen you sow seeds as tiny as the little black poppy seeds on your favorite bagel. Next you tend the fresh green shoots, and then you do some weeding. That's only a start, I know. But it's enough. It's enough in that it's a microcosm of the future. (As little, so big.) And it's enough in that you're joining multitudes of Great Workers who, taking responsibility for their own seed beds, join you. A word to Benjamin from *A Canticle for Leibowitz* could go on your wall: "To sense [your] responsibility is wisdom, Benjamin. To think you can carry it alone is folly." You need not, cannot, carry it alone, and you shouldn't try.

But action is indispensable. To take action is the antidote to Anthropocene anxiety, anxiety that otherwise slips into depression.

Through it all, don't forget the paradox you are. Our past shortcomings and mistakes, some of them doozies, are real. Blemished is who we are and who you will be too. Yet magnificence is yours as well. Grandma Nyla's favorite prayer has it right.

O God
Help me to believe
the truth about myself—
no matter how beautiful it is!

We can tell you how beautiful it is. Spud was in his crib, supposedly on his way to sleep but jabbering on, now with the complete sentences that come when a two-year-old is ambling toward three. Your dad was nearby, but Martín was in his own world and said to no one in particular, "I love Grandpa so much." We should all believe such unsolicited truth about ourselves, no matter how beautiful it is. On our better days, we do.

You've heard me say that my worldview is one of tragedy. Yet life with Nyla is graced at every turn, and never have

I felt so much gratitude or satisfaction as I do now. Tragedy sits alongside a deeply felt conviction that the existence of the universe is utterly astonishing, with life a miracle. I love Emily Dickinson's line: "To live is so startling it leaves little time for everything else." Life's miracle and mystery bring serenity and surprise. Thus does my tragic view partner with a somewhat unexpected giddy love of life. Or, rather, a giddy love of unexpected life.

Is it different for you?

I close with a rabbi and then add to Grandma's poem a favorite of mine and some wisdom from earlier. Love gets the last word all around.

The old rabbi says, "I am dust and ashes." He also says, "The world was made for me." So humble are we and so magnificent. See what your friends say if you put "We are dust and ashes" on your backpacks, right above "The world was made for me."

I've cited a favorite poem often, but never have I felt its force the way I feel it now. It's from Denise Levertov's collection *Candles in Babylon*. Earlier I wrote that we are now both the ark and the flood, the exiled and the exilers. Babylon is where we've exiled ourselves; Babylon is us. But Levertov's poem itself is "Beginners." How apt is that for re-mappers and re-makers! The poet's words, like the prophet's, are for you. Note the use of "love," "imagine," "hope," "justice," and "mercy" in the very first lines. They rise to the top, like heavy cream, for such a time as this.

Beginners
But we have only begun to love the earth. We have only
    begun to imagine the fullness of life.
How could we tire of hope!—so much is in bud.

How can desire fail?—we have only begun to imagine
justice and mercy,
*Only begun to envision how it might be to live as siblings with
beast and flower, not as oppressors.*
Surely our river cannot already be hastening into the sea of
nonbeing?
Surely it cannot drag, in the silt, all that is innocent!
Not yet, not yet—there is too much broken that must be
mended,
*Too much hurt that we have done to each other that cannot yet
be forgiven.*
We have only begun to know the power that is in us if we
would join our solitudes in the communion of struggle.
*So much is unfolding that must complete its gesture, so much is
in bud.*

Add Niebuhr's wisdom to Levertov's inspiration, with this
preface: Your worst tragedy as "beginners" would be to have no
sense of tragedy. Lacking its realism and lacking action, you will
fall into despair. Grab hold of the saving alternative, namely
fragments that reflect the whole. Here's Niebuhr's:

Nothing that is worth doing can be achieved in our
lifetime; therefore we must be saved by hope. Nothing
which is true or beautiful or good makes complete sense
in any immediate context of history; therefore we must
be saved by faith. Nothing we do, however virtuous, can
be accomplished alone; therefore we are saved by love.
No virtuous act is quite as virtuous from the standpoint of our friend or foe as it is from our standpoint.

Therefore we must be saved by the final form of love which is forgiveness.

Above all, keep saying "yes to life in spite of everything" and "I love you so much." (Don't forget the birds. Or your carrots.)

With hovering love,
Grandpa and Grandma

P.S. I have a request. If by the time you read this as young men, I am dead, as dead I well may be, would you two join your mother's lovely voice—maybe your dad's too—at my memorial service? And would you sing not just any song; rather, this one, where your living and my dying meet in a love that casts out fear and is stronger than death? It even bridges geological epochs.

Pues si vivimos, para Dios vivimos
Y si morimos, para Dios morimos.
Sea que vivamos o que muramos,
Somos del buen Dios, somos del buen Dios.

In all our living, we belong to God;
and in our dying, we are still with God;
So, whether living, or whether dying,
we belong to God; we belong to God.

ACKNOWLEDGMENTS

Though I carry responsibility for these letters, they're from both Nyla and me. She has read them all, we have discussed them, and changes have been made. Andy Rasmussen and Lina Villegas-Palaez, parents to the grandsons, have also graciously responded to many of them.

I've not been shy about asking help from friends Lisa Dahill, Melanie Harris, Cynthia Moe-Lobeda, Cláudio Carvalhaes, Wes Granberg-Michaelson, Gary Dorrien, Richard Crouter, Peter Smith, Daniel Spencer, Tom Christensen, Dennis Ormseth, Janet Parker, Aana Vigen, Paul Santmire, Nahum Ward-Lev, Roger Gottlieb, Carmen Ratzlaff, Victoria Loorz, and Paul and Rene Wee. All read letters or parts of letters when I needed counsel.

Some letters have been shared at conferences or in university and seminary classes of which I've been part.

The dedication is to our grandsons in the first instance but also to others who've let us adopt them as bonus grandchildren and who consider us their bonus grandparents. We love them all. We've also become grandparents to a dog. Grandparenthood is fast approaching a full-time blessing.

Special thanks go to Lil Copan and Jana Riess. I've long wanted—and needed—such editors. I am grateful.

Larry Rasmussen

Santa Fe, August 1, 2021

FOR FURTHER READING

Angelou, Maya. *On the Pulse of Morning: An Inaugural Poem*. New York: Random House, 1993.

Baldwin, James. *The Price of the Ticket: Collected Nonfiction, 1948–1985*. New York: St. Martin's Press, 1985.

Berry, Thomas. *The Great Work: Our Way into the Future*. New York: Bell Tower, 1999.

Birch, Bruce C., Jacqueline E. Lapsley, Cynthia Moe-Lobeda, and Larry L. Rasmussen. *Bible and Ethics in the Christian Life: A New Conversation*. Minneapolis: Fortress Press, 2018.

Bonhoeffer, Dietrich. *Letters and Papers from Prison*. Dietrich Bonhoeffer Works. Volume 8. Minneapolis: Fortress Press, 2009.

Dorrien, Gary. *Breaking White Supremacy: Martin Luther King, Jr. and the Black Social Gospel*. New Haven: Yale University Press, 2018.

Frankl, Victor E. *Yes to Life: In Spite of Everything*. Boston: Beacon Press, 2020.

Glaude Jr., Eddie L. *Begin Again: James Baldwin's America and Its Urgent Lessons for Our Own*. New York: Crown, 2020.

Greene, Brian. *Until the End of Time: Mind, Matter, and Our Search for Meaning in an Evolving Universe*. New York: Alfred A. Knopf, 2020.

Harari, Yuval Noah. *Homo Deus: A Brief History of Tomorrow*. London: Vintage Books, Penguin Random House, 2015.

Harris, Melanie L. *Ecowomanism: African-American Women and Earth-Honoring Faiths*. Maryknoll, NY: Orbis Books, 2017.

Heschel, Abraham J. *The Prophets: An Introduction*. New York: Harper Torchbooks, 1962.

Isaacson, Walter. *Einstein: His Life and Universe*. New York: Simon and Schuster, 2007.

Kimmerer, Robin Wall. *Braiding Sweetgrass: Indigenous Wisdom, Scientific Knowledge, and the Teachings of Plants*. Minneapolis: Milkweed Editions, 2013.

Lewis, Simon L., and Mark A. Maslin. *The Human Planet: How We Created the Anthropocene*. New Haven: Yale University Press, 2018.

Niebuhr, Reinhold. *Moral Man and Immoral Society*. New York: Charles Scribner's Sons, 1932.

Rasmussen, Larry. *Earth-honoring Faith: Religious Ethics in a New Key*. New York: Oxford University Press, 2013.

Sittler, Joseph. *Evocations of Grace: Writings on Ecology, Theology, and Ethics*. Edited by Steven Bouma-Prediger and Peter Bakken. Grand Rapids, MI: Eerdmans, 2000.

Ward-Lev, Nahum. *The Liberating Path of the Hebrew Prophets: Then and Now*. Maryknoll, NY: Orbis Books, 2019.

NOTES

EPOCH TIMES

is climate stability... From an address by Larry Rasmussen, available at https://issuu.com/luthercollegepublications/docs/agora, Spring 2014.

the only period as stable as our own is our own... Elizabeth Kolbert, *Under a White Sky: The Nature of the Future* (New York: Crown, 2021), 196. Italics added.

as hot as this one... David Wallace-Wells, *The Uninhabitable Earth: A Story of the Future* (New York: Crown, 2019), 221.

This beautiful broken country... Terry Tempest Williams, email message to author, December 2015.

I think it pisses God off... Alice Walker, *The Color Purple* (New York: Pocket Books, 1982), 178.

Even a wounded world... Robin Wall Kimmerer, *Braiding Sweetgrass* (Minneapolis: Milkweed Editions, 2013), 327.

because Earth offers love... Kimmerer, *Braiding Sweetgrass*, 327.

between calamity and wisdom... David Grinspoon, *Earth in Human Hands: Shaping Our Planet's Future* (New York: Grand Central Publishing, 2016), xx.

in three million years... Data on warming and CO_2 concentrations as reported in Mark Kaufman, *Science*, "June Was the Warmest June Ever Recorded, but There's a Bigger Problem," Yahoo.com, July 16, 2019. https://www.yahoo.com/now/june-warmest-june-ever-recorded-100000992.html

melting at record rates... Kaufman, "June Was the Warmest," July 16, 2019.

from womb to tomb... With gratitude to Katilau Mbindyo and her work for the Climate Ethics class, Union Theological Seminary, New York City, Spring Semester, 2018.

for the future we desire... Quoted in Adam Vaughan, "Earth Day: Scientists Say 75% of Known Fossil Fuel Reserves Must Stay in Ground," *Guardian*, April 22, 2015. https://www.theguardian.com/environment/2015/apr/22/earth-day-scientists-warning-fossil-fuels

of the atmosphere as well... Neela Banerjee, "Appeals Court Takes Up Youth Climate Change Lawsuit Against Trump," *Inside Climate News*, November 20, 2017.

and the stars love us back... As passed along by John Grim in the Climate Ethics class at Yale Divinity School, Spring Semester, 2018.

kaleidoscope of creation... From John Chryssavgis, "The Face of God in the World: Insights from the Orthodox Christian Tradition," in *Religion and Ecology*, edited by John Hart (Hoboken, NJ: Wiley Blackwell, 2017), 277.

would be good for the world... Wendell Berry, *The Long-Legged House* (New York: Ballantine Books, 1971).

render history as progress... Wallace-Wells, *The Uninhabitable Earth*, 210. Wallace-Wells lists these from a manifesto by Kingsnorth and Hine but does not supply bibliographic data. I have slightly modified the third myth.

TENDER YEARS

when you use them all, you die... Kathleen Norris, *Dakota: A Spiritual Geography* (New York: Houghton Mifflin, 1993), 20.

the mystic chords of memory... "The mystic chords of memory, stretching from every battle-field, and patriot grave, to every living heart and hearth-stone, all over this broad land, will yet swell the chorus of the Union, when again touched, as surely they will be, by the better angels of our nature." From Abraham Lincoln's First Inaugural Address, March 4, 1861.

human line that we are... Simon L. Lewis and Mark A. Maslin, *The Human Planet: How We Created the Anthropocene* (New Haven, CT: Yale University Press, 2018), 88.

all around the world via television... Barry Lopez, *Horizon* (New York: Alfred A. Knopf, 2019), 279.

staring at those footprints... Reported by David Farrier in his *Footprints: In Search of Future Fossils* (New York: Farrar, Straus and Giroux, 2020), 5.

SOMETHING TO WRITE HOME ABOUT

of the Indian subcontinent... Taken from *Smithsonian* magazine, February 8, 2018. Accessed at https://smithsonianmag.com on July 1, 2020.

making consistently bad choices... Richard Leakey is credited with saying this in an entry about him in the *Encyclopedia Britannica* and referring to his book with Roger Lewin, *The Sixth Extinction: Patterns of Life and the Future of Humankind* (1995). Accessed at britannica.com on July 8, 2021.

human tribes side by side... "Fossilized Skull May Add Species to Human Family Tree," *Santa Fe New Mexican*, June 27, 2021, D-4.

they all came from here... From Mary Evelyn Tucker's video interview with Carl Anthony in *Journey of the Universe Educational Series*, Disc 3. Available with supporting materials at www.JourneyoftheUniverse.org/Ed-Series

a scratch... Except for the story of Carl Anthony, the remainder of this discussion of origins is from Louise Leakey, "Is the Human Race in Danger of Becoming Extinct Soon?" *TED Talks* and *Huffington Post*, December 18, 2019. https://www.huffpost.com/entry/human-extinction_b_3543036

a different...community... Lewis and Maslin, *The Human Planet*, 66–67.

when I was thirty-one... Lewis and Maslin, *The Human Planet*, 247.

one lunatic fringe... Annie Dillard, *Pilgrim at Tinker Creek* (New York: HarperCollins, 1974), 146.

YOU FINISH THE STORY

raised by the river... Kimmerer, *Braiding Sweetgrass*, 22.

where all else was oppressive lockdown... See Nelson Mandela, *Long Walk to Freedom* (Randburg, South Africa: Macdonald Purnell, 1994), 502–3.

is being destroyed overnight... Dietrich Bonhoeffer, *Letters and Papers from Prison, Dietrich Bonhoeffer Works, Volume 8* (Minneapolis: Fortress Press, 2009), 387.

Man's Search for Meaning... Viktor E. Frankl, *Man's Search for Meaning* (Boston: Beacon Press, 1959). The original was published in 1946.

still has to be a meaning... Viktor Frankl, *Yes to Life: In Spite of Everything* (Boston: Beacon Press, 2020), 111–12.

wave goodbye to goodbye... From Poet Laureate Joy Harjo, *A Map to the Next World* (New York: W. W. Norton & Co., 2001), 123.

sooner rather than later... Kaufman, "June Was the Warmest," July 16, 2019.

evolutionary reset... Wallace-Wells, *The Uninhabitable Earth*, 3.

I got meaning in my life... Lizzie Widdicombe, "Greta Thunberg's Happy Crusade," *New Yorker*, April 8, 2021. https://www.newyorker.com/magazine/2021/04/19/greta-thunbergs-happy-crusade

to desist from it... From the Talmudic collection Pirke Avot 2:21. https://tcjewfolk.com/not-obligated-complete-task/

LOVE IN A TIME OF PLAGUE

less than a raindrop... Carl Zimmer, "The Secret Life of a Coronavirus," *New York Times Sunday Review*, February 28, 2021. https://www.nytimes.com/2021/02/26/opinion/sunday/coronavirus-alive-dead.html

I don't want to go there... Sometimes the version is: "If I am not allowed to laugh in heaven, I don't want to go there." Likely both are from Luther's *Table Talks,* but here they are found on brainyquote.com/quotes/martin_luther_151419

changed the world forever... Centers for Disease Control and Prevention, n.d. https://www.cdc.gov/flu/pandemic-resources/1918-commemoration/1918-pandemic-history.htm

no difference in the fare... Josiah Young, *No Difference in the Fare* (Grand Rapids, MI: Eerdmans, 1998).

do unto you... Wendell Berry, *Citizenship Papers: Essays* (Berkeley, CA: Counterpoint Press, 2003), 157.

what good mothers do... Kimmerer, *Braiding Sweetgrass*, 122.

creating beauty... Kimmerer, *Braiding Sweetgrass*, 123.

no sorrow like my sorrow... Lamentations 1:12b.

"LOVE WITH LEGS"

a broken society... "To Live and Love with a Dying World," a conversation between Tim DeChristopher and Wendell Berry in *Orion* (Spring 2020): 14–21. https://orionmagazine.org/article/to-live-and-love-with-a-dying-world/

how Cornel West describes justice... Cornel West, Serene Jones, and Gary Dorrien on *Bill Moyers Journal*, July 3, 2009. http://www.pbs.org/moyers/journal/07032009/profile.html

the gravity of stark facts ... Abraham J. Heschel, *The Prophets: An Introduction* (New York: Harper Torchbooks, 1962), 9.

for such a time as this... Esther 4:14.

and Greta Thunberg... For a selection of her speeches, see Greta Thunberg, *No One Is Too Small to Make a Difference* (New York: Penguin Books, 2018).

wail an octave higher... Heschel, *The Prophets*, xi.

an alternative future... Nahum Ward-Lev, *The Liberating Path of the Hebrew Prophets: Then and Now* (Maryknoll, NY: Orbis Books, 2019), 11.

a great love... Ward-Lev, *The Liberating Path of the Hebrew Prophets*, 11.

the speed the love of God walks... Kosuke Koyama, *Three Mile an Hour God* (London: SCM Press, 1979), 7. Thanks to Wesley Granberg-Michaelson for bringing this to my attention in his book *Without Oars: Casting Off into a Life of Pilgrimage* (Minneapolis: Broadleaf Books, 2020), 21.

the power of anger... Beverly Wildung Harrison, "The Power of Anger in the Work of Love: Christian Ethics for Women and Other Strangers," *Union Seminary Quarterly Review* 36 (1981): 41–57.

four times as likely... Jenna Wortham, "A 'Glorious Poetic Rage,'" *New York Times Sunday Review*, June 7, 2020. https://www.nytimes.com/2020/06/05/sunday-review/black-lives-matter-protests-floyd.html

all beings would flourish... Ward-Lev, *The Liberating Path of the Hebrew Prophets*, 11.

anticipatory communities... Larry Rasmussen, *Earth-honoring Faith: Religious Ethics in a New Key* (New York: Oxford University Press, 2013), 227.

and reorder possibilities... Rasmussen, *Earth-honoring Faith*, 227.

oriented to the common good... Rasmussen, *Earth-honoring Faith*, 227.

courageously reveal and name oppression... The plumb line image is that of the prophet Amos in chapter 7: 7–9.

hearts will be changed... King quoted in Kelly Brown Douglas, "How Do We Know Black Lives Matter to God?" *The Christian Century*, September 30, 2020. https://www.christiancentury.org/article/how-my-mind-has-changed/how-do-we-know-black-lives-matter-god

always in process together... Bruce C. Birch, Jacqueline E. Lapsley, Cynthia Moe-Lobeda, and Larry L. Rasmussen, *Bible and Ethics in the Christian Life: A New Conversation* (Minneapolis: Fortress Press, 2018), 104.

ecological-economic vocation... Cynthia D. Moe-Lobeda, *Resisting Structural Evil: Love as Ecological-Economic Vocation* (Minneapolis: Fortress Press, 2013).

will have discovered fire... Teilhard de Chardin, *Toward the Future* (New York: Houghton Mifflin, 1936), XI, 86–87.

THE KINDNESS OF MICROBIAL STRANGERS

a disease everywhere... David Quammen, "Why Weren't We Ready for the Coronavirus?" *New Yorker*, May 4, 2020. https://www.newyorker.com/magazine/2020/05/11/why-werent-we-ready-for-the-coronavirus. Quammen is quoting Ali Khan, dean of the College of Public Health at the University of Nebraska Medical Center in Omaha.

all that participates in being... H. Richard Niebuhr, *The Purpose of the Church and Its Ministry* (New York: Harper & Row, 1956), 38.

the better part of life is microbial... Rob Dunn, *A Natural History of the Future*. New York: Basic Books, 2021, p. 238.

the immensity of the universe... This draws from John Philip Newell, *Sacred Earth, Sacred Soul* (New York: HarperCollins, 2021), 234.

sperm whales teaching family values... Carl Safina, "Mother Culture: For Sperm Whales, Family Is Paramount," *Orion*, May 19, 2020. https://orionmagazine.org/article/mother-culture/

THE CORE KEEPS SCORE

bodies, behaviors, and brains... Steve Brusatte, "Welcome to the Ruthless, Cutthroat World of Paleoanthropology," *New York Times Book Review*, January 3, 2021. https://www.nytimes.com/2020/12/22/books/review/fossil-men-kermit-pattison-the-sediments-of-time-maeve-leakey.html

in spite of everything... Frankl, *Yes to Life*.

will be planetary refugees... Abrahm Lustgarten, "The Great Climate Migration," *New York Times Magazine*, July 23, 2020. https://www.nytimes.com/interactive/2020/07/23/magazine/climate-migration.html?searchResultPosition=1

the bright threads... The discussion of "résumé" virtues and values and "eulogy virtues" and "legacy values" is from David Brooks, "The Moral Bucket List," *New York Times*, April 11, 2015. https://www.nytimes.com/2015/04/12/opinion/sunday/david-brooks-the-moral-bucket-list.html *with equanimity and humor...* Cited in Walter Isaacson, *Einstein: His Life and Universe* (New York: Simon and Schuster, 2007), 519–20.

not just a grab-bag candy game... Toni Morrison interview, *O: The Oprah Magazine*, November 2003. https://www.oprah.com/omagazine/Toni-Morrison-Talks-Love/4

for one's community... Ruth Bader Ginsburg, the 2017 Rathbun Lecture on a Meaningful Life. https://www.rev.com/blog/transcripts/ruth-bader-ginsburg-stanford-rathbun-lecture-transcript-2017

WE/THEY R US

than we can ever think... Michael Crofoot as cited in Sam Bingham, *The Last Ranch* (New York: Pantheon Books 1996), 345, emphasis in the original.

we may scorn and revile everything... Abraham Joshua Heschel, *I Asked for Wonder* (New York: Crossroads Publishing Co, 2008), 20.

as Nelson Mandela said... Mandela, *The Long Walk to Freedom.*

that did not practice love... Paraphrased from the Dedication to Barry Lopez in *Orion: People and Nature* (Spring 2021): 4.

ALL TOO HUMAN

G. K. Chesterton... *London Times*, January 14, 1918.

a people's way of life... This description of culture draws upon Joseph Henrich, *The WEIRDest People in the World* (New York: Farrar, Straus and Giroux, 2020), 15–18.

most adaptable to change... Dan Western, ed., *40 Inspirational Charles Darwin Quotes*, WealthyGorilla.com, n.d. Accessed October 29, 2021.

don't get a cookie for reducing it... From Layla F. Saad, *Me and White Supremacy: Combat Racism, Change the World, and Become a Good Ancestor* (Naperville, IL: Sourcebooks, 2020), 155.

changing themselves, or the world... James Baldwin, "White Man's Guilt," reprinted in *Black on White: Black Writers on What It Means to Be White*, edited by David R. Roediger (New York: Schocken Books, 1998), 321. The original was in *Ebony Magazine.*

to take responsibility... Willis Jenkins, *The Future of Ethics: Sustainability, Social Justice, and Religious Creativity* (Washington, DC: Georgetown University Press, 2013), 17.

DIFFERENT ALL THE SAME

the commonest thing going... Richard Powers, *The Time of Our Singing* (London: Penguin Random House, 2003), 484.

bipeds with the giant dreams... Diane Ackerman, "Worlds within Worlds," *New York Times*, December 4, 1995. https://www.nytimes.com/1995/12/17/opinion/worlds-within-worlds.html

how we are who we are... This section on symbolic consciousness draws on the discussion in Larry Rasmussen, *Earth-honoring Faith* (New York: Oxford University Press, 2013), 23–30. Readers can find a more extensive treatment there.

chimps become individuals, too... Jane Goodall in an interview with Krista Tippett, "The Shadow of Humanity and the Spirit of Animals," *Orion*, August 20, 2020. https://orionmagazine.org/article/the-shadow-of-humanity-and-the-spirit-of-animals/

are the creations... Brian Greene, *Until the End of Time: Mind, Matter, and Our Search for Meaning in an Evolving Universe* (New York: Alfred A. Knopf, 2020), 3, 8, 16.

complex...and exploratory minds... Greene, *Until the End of Time*, 9.

empathize with family members who suffer... An Elephant Funeral. *journeys-discoveringafrica.com/an-elephant-funeral*

WHAT'S IN A NAME IF THE NAME IS GOD?

and knows God... 1 John 4:7.

most unheard-of marvels... St. Augustine, *City of God*, translated by Henry Bettenson (New York: Modern Library Classics, 2000), I, 10:12.

shattered in a moment... Augustine, *City of God*, 138.

a smiling place... St. Augustine, Sermon 169.4.

toward the ineffable... Citation of Morrison by editors, *The Christian Century*, "Looking to Advent as We Grieve Our Covid-19 Dead," December 1, 2020. https://www.christiancentury.org/article/editors/looking-advent-we-grieve-our-covid-19-dead. The original is part of Morrison's lecture upon receiving the Nobel Prize for Literature in 1993.

will seem yours to exploit... Gregory Bateson, *Steps to an Ecology of Mind* (New York: Random House, 1972), 472.

all creatures are sacraments... Paul Santmire in *Celebrating Nature by Faith* (Eugene, OR: Wipf & Stock, 2020), 59, drawing upon a dissertation on Luther and "all creatures are sacraments" written by Russ Kleckley. Kleckley, "*Omnes Creaturae Sacramenta:* Creation, Nature, and World View in Luther's Theology of the Lord's Supper" (PhD diss., Ludwig-Maximilians-Universitaet Muenchen, Evangelisch-Theologische Fakultaet, 1990).

has got to be restructured... Bateson, *Steps to an Ecology of Mind*, 472. Emphasis in the original.

COMING OF AGE

of the European... Dietrich Bonhoeffer, "The Right to Self-Assertion," *Dietrich Bonhoeffer Works, English Edition* 11: 252.

in the name of freedom without constraint... With thanks to Jean Bethke Elshtain, in a conference address on Bonhoeffer and King.

something to conquer through technology... Dietrich Bonhoeffer, "Outline for a Book," *Letters and Papers from Prison*, DBWE 8: 500.

not some far-off infinite power... From Bonhoeffer, "Outline for a Book," *Letters and Papers from Prison*, DBWE 8: 501.

and light years... Joseph Sittler, *Evocations of Grace* (Grand Rapids, MI: Eerdmans, 2000), 77.

THE UNCONTAINED GOD

support of such views... Walter Isaacson, *Einstein, His Life and Universe* (New York: Simon and Schuster, 2007), 389.

a devoutly religious man... Isaacson, *Einstein*, 387.

religion without science is blind... Isaacson, *Einstein*, 390.

in the visible universe... Frank Wilczek, cited in *New York Times Book Review*, February 21, 2021, 15, in the review by Nell Freudenberger of Wilczek's *Fundamentals: Ten Keys to Reality*.

the little god... Farrier's title for his chapter on microbial life, *Footprints*, p. 249ff., borrowing from the Roman poet Ovid's *Metamorphoses*.

the zoo in you... Neil Shubin, *Your Inner Fish: A Journey into the 3.5 Billion-Year History of the Human Body* (New York: Random House, 2009), 173–78.

we were coming... Cited from Mani Lai Bhaumik, *Code Name God: The Spiritual Odyssey of a Man of Science* (India: Penguin Random House India Private Limited, 2018), 164.

The solidity of rocks... This is the literal rendering of the Irish text cited by John Philip Newell in *Sacred Earth, Sacred Soul* (San Francisco: HarperOne, 2021), 73.

a whopping 70 percent... Cited from Mani Lai Bhaumik, *Code Name God*, 159.

so many keywords... This discussion draws freely from Bhaumik, *Code Name God*.

a self that relates and knows... This paragraph and the preceding one draw from BJ Miller, "What Is Death?" *New York Times Sunday Review*, December 20, 2020: 4.

someone more naïve... Isaacson, *Einstein*, 388.

image of Paradise... Cited with permission from St. Vladimir's Press.

the luminous figure of the Nazarene... Isaacson, *Einstein*, 386.

DEMOCRACY ENDANGERED

feels like oppression... From the discussion in Ezra Klein, *Why We're Polarized* (New York: Avid Reader Press, 2020), 119.

a helluva drug... Jonathan Capehart, on the Brooks and Capehart segment of *PBS News*, October 29, 2021.

how many would choose whiteness... Isabel Wilkerson, *Caste: The Origins of Our Discontents* (New York: Penguin Random House, 2020), 352.

fragile, impermanent things... This citation and the following discussion draw from Ben Ehrenreich, "How Do You Know When Society Is About to Fall Apart?" *New York Times Magazine*, November 4, 2020. https://www.nytimes.com/2020/11/04/magazine/societal-collapse.html

750 military bases in eighty countries... Geoffrey Wheatcroft, "America's Dismal Foreign Policy—And What to Do About It," *New York Times Book Review*, August 7, 2021. https://www.nytimes.com/2021/08/07/books/review/after-the-apocalypse-andrew-bacevich.html

larger-than-life challenges... Ehrenreich, "How Do You Know When Society Is About to Fall Apart?"

for an extended time... Jared Diamond, *Collapse: How Societies Choose to Fail or Succeed* (New York: Viking, 2005), 3.

eight processes... Diamond, *Collapse*, 6.
Earth's photosynthetic capacity... Diamond, *Collapse*, 7.
undermining of... key values... Diamond, *Collapse*, 7.

DEMOCRACY ENHANCED

atop a darkened Capitol... The cover of *New Yorker*, January 19, 2021.
if its quantity is inordinate... Reinhold Niebuhr, *Moral Man and Immoral Society* (New York: Charles Scribner's Sons, 1932), 164. Italics mine.
and it never will... Frederick Douglass, "West India Emancipation," August 3, 1857, address in Canandaigua, New York, available at http://www.blackpast.org
from imbalances of power... My distillation from Reinhold Niebuhr's discussion of justice and power in *Christianity and Power Politics* (New York: Charles Scribner's Sons, 1940), 104.
to extend their [protected] rights... A deduction of Niebuhr's discussion of "The Preservation of Moral Values in Politics," *Moral Man and Immoral Society*, 231–56.
imperiling the peace... Niebuhr, *Moral Man and Immoral Society*, 129.
the matrix for achieving the common good... My formulation of Niebuhr's defense of democracy in Reinhold Niebuhr, *The Children of Light and the Children of Darkness* (New York: Charles Scribner's Sons, 1944).
fortunate few dominate the rest... The phrase is Jeffrey Stout's in *Blessed Are the Organized: Grassroots Democracy in America* (Princeton: Princeton University Press, 2010), xv.
makes democracy necessary... Niebuhr, *The Children of Light and the Children of Darkness*, xiii.
powerful democracies tend toward naïveté... For full discussion of this, see Harry R. Davis and Robert C. Good, eds., *Reinhold Niebuhr on Politics* (New York: Charles Scribner's Sons 1960), *passim*.
intensifying the underlying power dynamics... A theme of the chapter The Religious Resources of the Individual for Social Living, Niebuhr, *Moral Man and Immoral Society*, 51–82.
self-assertion in terms of the absolute... Niebuhr, *Moral Man and Immoral Society*, 64.
on Christian nationalist websites... "'A Place to Fund Hope': How Proud Boys and Other Fringe Groups Found Refuge on a Christian

Fundraising Website," *Washington Post*, January 18, 2021. https://washingtonpost.com/investigations/a-place-to-find-hope2021/01/18

forms of religious faith... Niebuhr, *The Children of Light and the Children of Darkness*, 130.

which all history justifies... Niebuhr, *Moral Man and Immoral Society*, 253. Italics mine.

through violent rebellion... Niebuhr, *Moral Man and Immoral Society*, 252.

non-violent coercion and resistance... Niebuhr, *Moral Man and Immoral Society*, 250.

without destroying them... Niebuhr, *Moral Man and Immoral Society*, 251.

against its oppressors... Niebuhr, *Moral Man and Immoral Society*, 252.

an equally efficacious weapon... Niebuhr, *Moral Man and Immoral Society*, 254.

developing non-violent resistance... Niebuhr, *Moral Man and Immoral Society*, 254.

fundamental economic relationships... Cited from James Cone, *Martin & Malcolm in America* (Maryknoll, NY: Orbis Books, 1991), 224.

until [whites] are free... Baldwin, "The Fire Next Time: Letter to My Nephew on the One Hundredth Anniversary of the Emancipation Proclamation," reprinted in *The Price of the Ticket*, 332. Incidentally, "the fire next time," the title of a famous work of Baldwin's, is from a slave song, "And God gave Noah the rainbow sign, No more water. The fire next time." Baldwin saw the condition of African Americans, as well as their emancipation, in apocalyptic terms.

the multitudes in your own bodies... Neil Shubin, *Your Inner Fish: A Journey into the 3.5 Billion-Year History of the Human Body* (New York: Random House, 2009), 18–19.

AFTERTIME

biodiversity's downward spiral... From Take Flight in *New Mexico Magazine*, "A Guide to Birding," April 7, 2021. https://www.newmexicomagazine.org

extend the hurricane season... Sarah Kaplan, "How Climate Change Helped Make Hurricane Ida One of Louisiana's Worst," *Washington Post*, August 30, 2021. https://www.washingtonpost.com/climate-environment/2021/08/29/how-climate-change-helped-make-hurricane-ida-one-louisianas-worst/

create their own weather… Henry Fountain, "How Bad Is the Bootleg Fire? It's Generating Its Own Weather," *New York Times*, July 19, 2021. https://www.nytimes.com/2021/07/19/climate/bootleg-wildfire-weather.html?action=click&module=RelatedLinks&pgtype=Article

the combined weight of all other creatures… John Green, *The Anthropocene Reviewed: Essays on a Human-Centered Planet* (New York: Dutton, 2021), 64–65.

free of human activity… Reported by Claw and Order in *New York Review of Books*, Vol. LXVIII, No. 17, November 4, 2021: 4.

at risk of extinction… PBS Newshour, September 10, 2020, reporting on *The Dasgupta Review on the Economics of Biodiversity*, accessed at https://www.pbs.org

harmony of economy and ecology… "Prosperity comes at 'devastating' cost to nature," Helen Briggs reporting for the BBC on *The Dasgupta Review on the Economics of Biodiversity*, commissioned by the UK Treasury in 2019 and directed by Professor Sir Partha Dasgupta, University of Cambridge, UK.

can be relapses… From Jesse Green, "Walt Whitman, Poet of a Contradictory America," *New York Times Style Magazine*, September 14, 2020. https://www.nytimes.com/2020/09/14/t-magazine/walt-whitman-cover.html

after the fall… Eddie L. Glaude, Jr., *Begin Again: James Baldwin's America and Its Urgent Lessons for Our Own* (New York: Crown, 2020), 16.

coming into view… Glaude, *Begin Again,* 16.

of the American story… Carlos Lozada, *What Were We Thinking* (New York: Simon and Schuster, 2020), 239.

shares the role with Death… E. B. White, *Here Is New York* (New York: The Little Bookroom, 1999), 54, from a description, mainly of Manhattan, in the summer of 1948.

collapse of a shareable world… Toni Morrison, "Home," in *The Source of Self-Regard: Selected Essays, Speeches, and Meditations* (New York: Alfred A. Knopf, 2019), 17.

for years to come… Lozada, *What Were We Thinking,* 239.

ELSEWHERE

and might yet be… The information about Maya Angelou is from *Wikipedia*, accessed online September 27, 2020. Some is about the poem *On the Pulse of Morning.*

no hiding place... Maya Angelou, *On the Pulse of Morning* (New York: Random House, 1993), n.p.

too small for anything but love... William Sloane Coffin, "Blessing to Begin a New School Year," Yale University.

in all its magnificence... Thomas Berry, *The Great Work: Our Way into the Future* (Tyler, TX: Bell Tower Press, 1999), 1–2.

in a mutually beneficial manner... Berry, *The Great Work*, 3.

RESPONSIBLE BY DEGREES

have to get good at it... Stewart Brand, cited in Kolbert, *Under a White Sky*, 137.

with intelligent design... Yuval Noah Harari, *Homo Deus: A Brief History of Tomorrow* (New York: Vintage Books, 2015), 85–86.

much of anything... Cited by Kolbert in *Under a White Sky*, 139.

and microbial species across the globe... Farrier, *Footprints*, 251.

a whole no-analog future... Kolbert, *Under a White Sky*, 7–8.

and being responsible... Frankl, *Yes to Life*, 41.

to the end and in the end... Frankl, *Yes to Life*, 96–97.

sequestrations of greenhouse gases... Willis Jenkins, *The Future of Ethics* (Washington, DC: Georgetown University Press, 2013), 31.

human well-being is derivative... Thomas Berry, "The Ecozoic Era," The Annual Schumacher Lecture (Great Barrington, MA: The Schumacher Center, 1991), n.p.

a new mode of living... Lewis and Maslin, *The Human Planet*, 369.

have names and addresses... Utah Phillips as cited by George Zachariah, "Whose *Oikos* Is It, Anyway?" in *Decolonizing Eco-Theology*, edited by S. Lily Mendoza and George Zachariah (Eugene, OR: Pickwick Publications, 2022), 208.

only 10 percent of emissions... https://www.oxfam.org/en/press-releases/worlds-richest-10-produce-half-carbon-emissions

and disruptive climate change... Olúfémi O. Táíwò, "Climate Controllers," *New Yorker*, November 1, 2021: 79.

IT'S ALL IN THE PRONOUNS

we must be theirs... Kimmerer, *Braiding Sweetgrass*, 8.

it's all in the pronouns... Kimmerer, *Braiding Sweetgrass*, 58.

all flourishing is mutual... Kimmerer, *Braiding Sweetgrass*, 382.

if humanity suffers... Al Gore, "The Turning Point: New Hope for the Climate," *Rolling Stone*, June 18, 2014. http://www.rollingstone.com/politics/ news/the-turning-point-new-hope-for-the-climate-20140618?print+true

just to have a mountain... Cited by Naomi Klein, *This Changes Everything: Capitalism vs. the Climate* (New York: Simon and Schuster, 2014), 337.

the ravaging of nature... James Cone, "Whose Earth Is It, Anyway?" in *Earth Habitat: Eco-Injustice and the Church's Response*, edited by Dieter Hessel and Larry Rasmussen (Minneapolis: Fortress Press, 2001), 23.

defense of white world supremacy... Cone, "Whose Earth Is It, Anyway?", 23.

in our discussions, decisions, and actions... Cited in Larry Rasmussen, "From Social Justice to Creation Justice in the Anthropocene," in *The Wiley Blackwell Companion to Religion and Ecology*, edited by John Hart (Hoboken, NJ: John Wiley & Sons, Inc.), 240.

to sustain those who sustain us... Kimmerer, *Braiding Sweetgrass*, 382.

to its responsibility... Kimmerer, *Braiding Sweetgrass*, 311.

thanks to the waters... All the quotations of these pages from The Thanksgiving Address are available in numerous publications in various languages, often under the title "The Haudenosaunee Thanksgiving Address." I have used the 1993 Six Nations Museum publication.

any way we wish... Cited from Kolbert, *Under a White Sky*, 116.

BECOMING GOOD ANCESTORS

between your birth date and death date... Michael Curry with Sara Grace, *Love Is the Way: Holding on to Hope in Troubling Times* (New York: Avery, 2020), 97.

your one wild and precious life... Mary Oliver, "The Summer Day," *House of Light* (Boston: Beacon Press, 1990).

because we ran out of stones... Attributed to the former Saudi oil minister Sheik Ahmed Zaki Yamani.

and inner journey... These elements are my adaptation from the discussion of John Grim and Mary Evelyn Tucker, *Ecology and Religion* (Washington, DC: Island Press, 2014), 37–42.

ice age cycle... Clive Hamilton, *Defiant Earth: The Fate of Humans in the Anthropocene* (Cambridge: Polity Press, 2017), ix.

NOTES

loving and just world... GreenFaith, "Our Vision," n.d. https://greenfaith.
org/about/

the glory of God is humanity fully alive... Irenaeus (ca. 140–202) in *Against
Heresies*, published as Vol. 1 of *The Ante-Nicene Fathers* (Grand Rapids,
MI: Eerdmans, 1952), 180.

this primordial communion... I draw from my discussion of Berry and
Swimme, *The Universe Story*, p. 70, in Larry Rasmussen, *Earth Community, Earth Ethics* (Orbis Books, 1996), 29.

core of every community's life... Rita Nakashima Brock and Rebecca Parker,
*Saving Paradise: How Christianity Traded Love of This World for Crucifix-
ion and Empire* (Boston: Beacon Press, 2008), 418.

values and relationships... Brock and Parker, *Saving Paradise*, 418.

of the forest and its life, and humans... The litany was written by Lisa Dahill.
I am grateful she shared it for this letter. A full account of the community that gathered, the ritual, and reflection upon it is available. See Lisa
E. Dahill, "Lent, Lament, and the River: Interfaith Ritual in the Ashes
of the Thomas Fire," *Liturgy*, 34 (2019): 4–14. Access online at https://
doi.org/10.1080/0458063X.2019.1679578

whether I can bear... For a full account of this service, see Cláudio
Carvalhaes, "Why I Created a Chapel Service Where People Confess to Plants," sojo.net, September 26, 2019. https://sojo.net/articles
/why-i-created-chapel-service-where-people-confess-plants. Slightly
adapted, available at "Native Wisdom," http://www.rainbowbody.net/
Ongwhehonwhe/cherokee.htm

LEAVING A LEGACY

until it is faced... James Baldwin, "As Much Truth as One Can Bear," *New
York Times Book Review*, January 14, 1962.

Try anyway .... Barack Obama, *A Promised Land* (New York: Crown, 2020),
446. Emphasis in the original.

the true wonder... Maya Angelou, *A Brave and Startling Truth* (New York:
Random House, 1995), n.p.

change our children's birthright... Amanda Gorman, *The Hill We Climb*,
poem given at the Inauguration of President Joseph R. Biden, January
20, 2021.

212

NOTES

to think you can carry it alone is folly... Walter M. Miller, Jr., *A Canticle for Leibowitz* (New York: HarperCollins, 1959), 160.

no matter how beautiful it is... Poem of Macrina Wiederkehr in *Soul Weavings: A Gathering of Women's Prayers* (Minneapolis: Augsburg Publishing House, 1996), 62.

little time for anything else... The quotation is from *Letters of Emily Dickinson*, edited by Thomas H. Johnson (Cambridge, MA: Harvard University Press 1958).

so much is in bud... Denise Levertov, "Beginners," *Candles in Babylon* (New York: New Directions, 1982), 82–83. Used with permission.

the final form of love which is forgiveness... Reinhold Niebuhr, *The Irony of American History* (New York: Charles Scribner's Sons, 1962), 63.

bridges even geological epochs... Cf., "'For the mountains may move and the hills disappear, but even then my faithful love for you will remain. My covenant of blessing will never be broken,' says the Lord, who has mercy on you" (Isaiah 54:10, NLT).

which is forgiveness... Reinhold Niebuhr, *The Irony of American History* (New York: Charles Scribner's Sons, 1962), 63.

In all our living... "In All Our Living," *New Century Hymnal* (Nashville: United Methodist Publishing House), 499.